EDEN
TO EVIL

THE PUZZLE OF CREATION EXPLAINED

EXPOSING THE TRUTH OF ORIGINS & CREATION

GERRY BURNEY

EDEN TO EVIL

Copyright © 2016 by Gerry Burney

World Ahead Press is a division of WND Books. The views and opinions expressed in this book are those of the author and do not necessarily reflect the official policy or position or WND Books.

Paperback ISBN: 978-1-944212-36-0
eBook ISBN: 978-1-944212-37-7

Printed in the United States of America
16 17 18 19 20 21 LSI 9 8 7 6 5 4 3 2 1

Unless otherwise indicated, Bible quotations are taken from The King James Version. Copyright © 1999 by Zondervan.

Gerry Burney
Box 1299
Ukiah, Calif. 95482

www.TargetTruthMinistries.com
BurneyFam@prodigy.net

CONTENTS

INTRODUCTION

"**L**et no one in any way deceive you, for it (the end times), will not come unless the apostasy comes first" (2 Thess. 2:1–3; Matt. 24:10–12) What might be the signs of the apostasy?

A. *Jesus as fully God* is either not a priority discussed in church, or is even denied by some churches.

B. *The atonement of Christ*, as the *primary* message of the church, is replaced with a message primarily of good deeds and meeting human needs (poverty, environment, health care, tolerance, et cetera.).

C. *Separation of church and state*, as interpreted today (which was *not* the understanding of the founding fathers), seeks to *exclude* God from public life.

D. *Sex outside the marriage of one man and one woman*, is accepted by most people, even Christians. Marriage and divorce were *never* designed by God as a right, but rather to represent a state of being or status, and people cannot be given equal status in life by governments. Marriage and divorce *primarily* represent God's plan of salvation and judgment. See *Marriage & Divorce Study*—Target Truth Ministry.com).[67]

E. *Abortion* is accepted by society as a right by most people. Here, man becomes a god, determining when life begins. Fifty-six million babies have been killed since abortion was legalized. Ironically, this is double the number of illegal aliens the country seems to need in order to care for the generation which has aborted the babies.

F. *Euthanasia* (legal suicide), is accepted by many. Man, here, becomes a god, determining when life ends.

G. *Macroevolution* is worshiped in place of God. Man is elevated to the "highest form of life" by believing in macroevolution. Macroevolution is actually a religion, as it requires faith (there is *no* scientific proof, only a hypothesis). Additionally, scientific evidence (which actually *denies* macroevolution), has been *deleted* from so-called education.[65] Christianity, on the other hand, is *not* a religion—it is a relationship, and welcomes all evidence.

God's Word tells us that we are sinners at *conception*, and all have been condemned by God to hell, even *before* we are born. This is not because of our ancestor Adam's sin, as taught by many today (The Federal Headship Theory, or The Traducian Theory). Rather, it is because we each are individually, personally, responsible for our sin (*original sin*) in Eden (the *original* creation). God loves His creation. Therefore, God *predestined* a plan to reconcile with those who have fallen, if they will change and trust in Jesus. God *re*created this Earth (the seven-day event), to provide for this period of reconciliation.

This period of reconciliation includes Satan, who has also fallen. Satan imitates God in order to deceive many into rejecting Jesus and accepting false religions. Satan persuades many to have faith in science (which is based upon limited knowledge), and to accept human desires such as sex, wealth, health, fame, status, et cetera, as *priorities* in life, in order to detour our true need to trust in Christ, so as to avoid hell. There is a specific number of beings to be born into this flesh existence, and then God will usher in the end judgment. God will soon destroy this creation, and bring about a return to Eden (the new heaven and earth).

The apostasy is here and that number to be born will soon be reached. Israel is God's timepiece, and the clock was reset in 1948. The end times are upon us, and this more than likely is the generation to see Christ return, and the judgment take place. Don't be deceived by philosophies (religions) with no evidence to support their claims or understandings of life and death. A dialogue is good, but without the *truth*, dialoguing is worthless. Truth is exclusive. There can be only one truth. Those who point to so-called other truths, are uninformed (one of Satan's tactics), so please share these books, studies, and messages (available at *TargetTruthMinistries.com*), with others, to help inform the multitudes who are lost, spiritually weak, and heading to hell.

God has predestined a *millennium* to provide a way for those who (during this lifetime), haven't heard the call to Christ, in order to receive their opportunity for salvation. [66, 68] Only those who trust in Christ will avoid hell. Many in this life have been deceived by Satan's imitation faiths.[67]

If theology is not clear to you (even many theologians haven't figured out God's plan yet), and if you are concerned about the fate of humankind, your family, and neighbors, please share these books, studies, and messages on God's plan with them. These books and studies are for those who are searching God's

Word for the truth, and who are truly concerned with humankind's eternal state, whether it be heaven or hell. All will live eternally, either in the presence of their Creator, or separated to spend all eternity isolated, alone, forever in outer darkness. Satan even has people thinking that hell will either be a place where all beings will be grouped together to be able to make the best of the situation, or that hell doesn't really exist. However, God is clear: hell is eternal darkness (alone). Eternal torment is the justice determined for those who have sinned against their Creator, who is uncreated—eternal. We are *all* sinners, and *all* condemned, but God offers us reconciliation, and life with Him in His kingdom, if we will *trust* in Him.

Pastor Gerry Burney
P. O. Box 1299   www.TargetTruthMinistries.com
Ukiah, CA 95482   BurneyFam@prodigy.net

Please make tax-deductible donations payable to: **Crossroads Church/ Target Truth Ministry**, and mail to above address to help us spread the truth, or go online: PayPal—TargetTruthMinistries.com/Crossroads Church.

This ministry is dedicated to God's Word and providing scripturally based answers to theological questions that have puzzled scholars for hundreds of years. The result is a unique understanding using the whole of Scripture to reveal the truth (Daniel 12:4).

CHAPTER 1

THE PUZZLE OF GOD'S WORD

An understanding of the creation, and the beginning of our existence, is essential in understanding everything else that follows the creation, including our need for salvation and a Savior. For centuries, scholars and theologians have struggled to understand exactly how the two creation narratives of the 7-day, and Eden (which on the surface seem to be completely different), can both reflect God's creation. Some, over the centuries, have even suggested that one of these creation narratives is not from God, because they are so different in many ways. The truth of these two creation narratives lies in understanding how God speaks to us.

God speaks to us in riddles and parables, so that those who truly desire to know the truth will receive the truth. Jesus (fully God in the flesh), used riddles, or parables, in the New Testament (Matt. 13:9–17, 17:20). The God of the New Testament is the same God as the God of the Old Testament (One God and one Savior—Isa. 43:3, 11; 45:21–22). Some of these riddles or parables in the Old Testament include the story of Joseph (a typology of Jesus and salvation—Gen. 30 through 50), the rules for cleansing a leper (a typology of Jesus and salvation—Lev. 14:1–32), and the six cities of refuge (a typology of Jesus and salvation—Num. 35). Most of us believe in some kind of life after death, but have you ever thought about whether we existed *before* being born into this life, on this planet? This is not some pagan belief, like the Hindu belief of bodiless souls in the universe waiting for a body, or the Mormon belief in God producing spirit souls through sex. In God's Word, in Eph. 1:4–11; John 3:18; Romans 8:28–30; 2 Tim. 1:9; and 1 Peter 2:25, God tells us that He knew us *before* we came into this world. To help us understand this relationship with God (before being born), let's look at God's Word.

Jesus gave us three parables in Luke 15: the lost sheep, the lost coin, and the lost son. We should note first of all that in reading about these three situations (the shepherd who lost a sheep, a woman who lost a coin, and the father who lost one son), that the focus is not on the sheep, or the coin, or the lost son. The focus of the parables, Jesus tells us, is from the point of view of the one who was the owner of the sheep, and the owner of the coins, and the father of the lost son. In each parable, the owner is determined to be restored to the lost possession.

The point of these three parables is that God is patient, and waiting for the lost to return to Him. God is not quick to judge the Earth, He is patient. But, one day, God has promised the time will be up (Luke 21:24–32; Romans 11:25–26). Thank God He has waited this long in history.

In thinking about this first parable (the lost sheep), turn in your Bibles to Isaiah 53:6–7 and note that in the Old Testament, that Isaiah (writing 700 years before the birth of Christ) talks of the same thing—lost sheep. Also note, that this chapter of Isaiah also has a lot to say about the prophesy of the Messiah (Jesus). And, these prophesies were fulfilled by Jesus at His suffering and death.

In the first two parables, the shepherd and the woman are seen as frantically searching for that which they had lost. The lost items represented value, and they needed to find them, or lose them. These are parables about God recovering what has been lost (us). But, does God have to extend Himself to us because He needs us back, or does He do so out of His love for us?

God does not need us to complete His existence. God created us for His pleasure, not because He needs us. But, God loves us and is concerned with our being lost, and is patient in His plan to see us restored to a relationship with Him—to be reconciled.

In fact, God (Jesus) is willing to die for us. All of us, even though we are all sinners (Romans 3:10–12, 23), are valuable to God, and He desires that we all choose life (Deut. 30:19), and become "born again" (John 3:1–7). God wants to develop a relationship with us, spend time with us, and God wants us to develop a relationship with Him, and spend time with Him, so that no one remains lost and separated forever, permanently condemned to eternal separation—hell (John 3:18; 5:28–29).

We are each valuable to God, and He desires that we each be restored, or reconciled to Him. God says in Isaiah 55:7 that He will freely pardon us. In Luke 15:7 and 10, at the end of each of the first two parables, even though these parables are about sheep, and coins, Jesus tells us that the key to salvation is repenting (which is changing).

Now, sheep can change (they can obey, they can get sheared), and coins change when they deflate in value, but Jesus is talking about people. We must change from the world's ways (our ways), to God's ways (His ways). Repent (change).

So, these parables are about souls being restored to God (if they change). We read in John 1:1–18, and Phil. 2:5–8, about God extending Himself to us by taking on the form of flesh, so as to die for us, a perfect sacrificial price, to pay for our sins, so that those who trust in Him, and spend time with Him, will enjoy Paradise with Him. God loves the sinner, just not the sin (our bad actions). He is waiting patiently for us to return that love, that desire to spend time with Him, and deny the world's ways.

In the third parable, about the lost son, note that sin is seen here, as the son takes several steps to walk away from God (the Father). These steps include rebellion against the father, desire for total independence (separation from the father), waste of the inheritance, desperate need, and finally debasement and bondage.

But, just as there were certain steps away from the father, there are also certain steps back to be restored and reconciled. In Luke 15:17, we see him awakening to his condition. While he was on his way down, he undoubtedly said to himself that his hard times were only temporary, and that his metaphorical ship would soon come in. He imagined he still had friends. Even when he had to take a job with a detested pig farmer, he supposed he was only doing it on a short-term basis, until his bad fortune changed.

The first step back was *coming to his senses*. The second step back was making an honest confession of his sin. We read in verses 18 and 19 of Luke 15 that the son humbled himself. He did not use excuses or blame others. He openly admitted his sin. The third step was to return to the father (Luke 15:20–21). For us, this means being born again, spending time with God, and developing a relationship with Him.

There is another common theme of these three parables. They all refer to the *lost*. If you think about it, in order to be lost, one must have belonged to someone, or had a relationship with someone, *before* being lost. In these parables of Jesus He tells a story of the sheep existing with the shepherd, *before* being lost, the coins all being with the owner, *before* being lost, and, the son existing with the father, *before* being lost.

Throughout God's Word, He tells us that we need to be reconciled to Him to be saved; to be restored to His kingdom. Reconciled means to restore a relationship we once had, before being lost. Paul wrote in Romans 1:21 about when people *knew God*, indicating once again a relationship with God prior to this age we now live in.

In the context of Romans 1, Paul is pointing out how both Jew and Gentile (all nations) are fallen and separated from God, and therefore, we now don't know God as we once did. Since we are all born sinners, have fallen and are therefore separated from God at birth, this period of *knowing God* must have been in an age prior to this age we are birthed into now (Eden). We know from Psalm 51:5, and other places, that we are sinners at conception, even in the womb. We know from John 3:18, that we are all born condemned already. We are all sinners, and that is why Jesus did not come to condemn us, because we are already condemned.

So, yes, God foreknew us all, and we are all lost. All sinners. All separated from God at birth. And we all need to be reconciled. We all need to repent (change), be born again into a relationship with God, and spend time with Him. *OR*, remain condemned to hell, separated, isolated, for all eternity . . . alone.

God speaks to us in a riddle/parable concerning our origins. The 7-day creation account begins in Genesis 1:2, and the Eden creation account begins in Genesis 2:4. The original Hebrew was a continuous series of words. Chapters and verses came into use by the fifteenth century, and the divisions can be somewhat arbitrary. Can you figure out from the following statements which creation account actually occurs first *biblically* after the introduction of the creation? *A*, *B*, or, can they be combined as in *C*?

Genesis 1:1 - In the beginning God created the heaven (*singular*), and the earth (Rev. 21 - heaven (*singular*).

a. The 7-day Account Beginning in Genesis 1:2

The earth was formless (Genesis 1:2—However, in Isaiah 45:18 the earth was *not* created formless).

Days 2–5 – God creates three heavens (*plural*): The heaven of God's abode (Gen. 1:8; 2 Cor. 12:2, a *third* heaven). The heaven of the stars (Gen. 1:14–19). The heaven of the sky (Gen. 1:20–22).

First plants, and lastly mankind (Gen. 1:26–28).

All the host (multitudes and armies of beings), of *both* heaven and earth are completely finished (Gen. 2:1).

b. The Eden account beginning in Genesis 2:4

These are the generations of heaven (singular), and earth (Gen. 2:4).

God had not caused it to rain yet (Gen. 2:5–6). Earth here in Eden is formed, but not inhabited yet (in agreement with Isaiah 45:18—the earth was *not* created formless).

First mankind, and lastly plants and animals (Gen. 2:7).

Original sin (Gen. 3, which causes the host of Eden/heaven to be separated from God—Ezek. 31; Rev. 12:1–4).

c. Blending them together where Eden is part of Day 6:

The earth was formless (Gen. 1:2—However, in Isaiah 45:18—the earth was *not* created formless).

Day 2–5 – God creates three heavens (*plural*—see a).

Day 3 – God *planted the earth* with vegetation, plants, and trees (Gen. 1:11–13).

Day 6 – God made mankind to rule over plants and animals (Gen. 1:26–30). It is supposedly here on Day 6 that the Eden account explains mankind's creation (and the eventual fall), where *no plants or trees existed* (Day 3), until mankind had been created (Gen. 2:4–3:24—Day 6, Eden).

If you took time to check your Bible translation, you probably discovered that the word *heaven* (*singular*), appears as *heavens* (*plural*) in many translations in Genesis 1:1 today. However, the original Hebrew, as well as the first Greek translation from Hebrew to Greek (the Septuagint from 300 years before Jesus was born which Jesus used), translates *heaven* as singular, meaning that the 7-day creation (which describes three heavens), cannot be the creation referred to in Genesis 1:1, where God uses the singular *heaven*. In fact, the word *heaven* in Genesis 1:1 was not changed until the eighteenth century, well after the King James Version of the Bible. This word *heaven* was changed to more correctly fit the 7-day narrative, because supposedly, if God created three heavens in the 7-day event, God must have meant *heavens* (*plural*), in Genesis 1:1, and so mankind corrected God's supposed mistake.

But, God did *not* make a mistake! God has given us a riddle, a puzzle, to see who is searching His Word for the truth, and to see who has eyes to see which creation narrative came first—thus discovering our real need for salvation. God even made the answer so obvious, that *B* should jump out at us as the only possible correct option. The story is so simple. We were created, have fallen from our relationship with God, are born into this world lost, facing death, and in need of reconciliation (Romans 5:10–11), and a Savior. God so loves us that He came to us in the form of Jesus (John 3:16–21). See Appendix 2—Creation Comparison Chart.

Many insist that we are good people at our birth and we make mistakes. And, because we were once good, we are able to do good works and overcome our sins—in other words, we don't need a Savior unless we continue to be bad people. This philosophy is exactly how Islam, Buddhism, and may other faiths view our sin nature. Because the Christian church has neglected the creation story, we have allowed other faiths to claim that people can be good enough without a Savior, thus condemning millions to eternal separation from God and His kingdom. Even many Christian groups insist upon works, either performed by the individual or by the church, to prepare one for heaven. However, a correct understanding of our previous relationship with God will reveal to us our utter hopelessness without a Savior. This book will give those who want eyes to see the truth, and ears to hear the truth, the understanding of God's truth from God's Scripture, and not man's traditions.

One of the questions which arises when considering this understanding that we were all originally part of the creation in Eden, concerns our understanding about angels and Adam (mankind—actually *et-adam* in the Hebrew, meaning *mankind*). Obviously we are not angels (eternal), in this human flesh (mortal), and we have a hard time thinking of Adam (mankind—*et-adam*), as being in an angelic state originally as an angel.

Most of us have formed our opinion of what an angel is based upon stories we have been told, or books we have read, and traditions passed down to us. Exactly what does the word *angel* in the Bible mean to you? The word *angel* in the Bible is *not* a reference to a being created different from mankind (adam— actually *et-adam* in the Hebrew—mankind). The assumption is that angels were created differently than humans. However, the only references to the creation of the host of heaven is the creation story in Eden. God's purpose in the Bible is to describe the human story, our creation and fall with Satan, and God does not give details on the host of heaven that remain true to God.

The Hebrew word *angel* is a reference to the various *functions* assigned to a being who is created to serve God. Pastors and priests are angels (Rev. 2, 3), created to serve God—their *function* makes them *angels* (in the service of God), not their *appearance.* The Hebrew word *malak*, translated as *angel,* means ambassador, teacher, messenger, or deputy—referring to their function, not their physical makeup or appearance. The Greek word *aggelos,* translated as angel, means messenger, or pastor (Rev. 2, 3)—again referring to their function. The Greek word *isaggelos* means equal to or like the angels, used in Luke 20:36, where the passage states that in the resurrection we cannot die anymore because we will be like, or equal to, the angels—eternal.

In Psalm 148:1–6, we are all listed together as angels, or the host of creation. All beings are angels (all beings with different *functions*, created to serve God). All the host (all armies and nations), are angels (beings with various *functions*, created to serve God). All the sun, moon, and stars, symbolically, all the righteous, are beings with various functions, created to serve God. All the waters above heaven, symbolically, all those who remained true to God at the fall, and did not sin (Gen. 1:6–7), are the host of creation, beings with various *functions*, angels, created to serve God.

In Hebrews 2:5–18, Jesus was made temporarily lower than the angels (to be able to die), and we are compared as also being temporarily lower than the angels (condemned to die). The reason for this is so that salvation and reconciliation can take place for all of us who sinned in the past (Romans 5:12, because all sinned), and who now trust in Jesus. The saved will be resurrected to their eternal state of angelic function. In Hebrews 9:23–28, *copies* are not limited to temple implements, but also include the host of creation who have fallen, and are now cleansed by the perfect blood of Jesus, so as to be able to enter heaven. The context of *copies* in Hebrews 9 includes the many (v. 28), who are born flesh (*copies*), for salvation (vv. 19–21).

Adam was an angel in Eden (defined biblically as a being created to be eternal to *serve* God, a *function*). The only reference in the Bible to the creation of angels, or beings created to serve God, is in Genesis 2:4–3:24, where the host of heaven in Eden are first mentioned—mankind, Satan, and the cherubim, who were all created to serve God. Those in Eden are delineated by their function, not by their appearance. Satan's description as a serpent is symbolic of evil, not a literal physical description.

By the end of the 7-day creation narrative, note that *all* the host of *both* heaven and earth are finished (Gen. 2:1). Babies born today are not a brand new creation. Every baby represents one of God's created host, which fell in paradise, now entering this world (this age of Grace), for the purpose of reconciliation back to God. Note that Adam was a son of God (angelic/eternal—and became flesh/mortal), and we are sons of Adam (born flesh/mortal—Luke 3:38). Do not confuse this with the Mormon belief that through a "man god" having sex, that spirit babies were created to be born, or the Hindu belief in a cloud of spirits in the universe awaiting a body to possess, neither of which has any biblical support. Each of us are a result of the original creation by God in Eden (supernatural like Adam).

God speaks to us in His word in riddles and parables (Matt. 13:9–17, 17:20). Whether we are called *angels* (Rev. 1:20: Ps. 148:2) *people, or armies* (Gen. 2:1;

Ezek. 1:24; Rev. 19:14), *stars* (Rev. 12:1–2; Job 38:7), *host* (Gen. 2:1; Ps. 148:2), *trees* (Ezek. 31; Gen. 2:9), *stones* (Isaiah 14:19; Ezek. 28:14–16; Matt. 3:8–10; Luke 19:40; 1 Peter 2:4–5), *waters* (Rev. 17:15, 19:6; Ps. 148:4–6; Ezek. 1:24), or *sons of God* (Romans 8:14–19; Job 38:7), in Scripture—all are part of the host of creation. We were all created with a supernatural *body* in Eden, and simply assigned different *jobs* to serve God, which is the biblical definition of the term *angel*, not the definition we have invented today through traditions, and stories.

For a long time people believed the Earth was flat, only to find out later that it was round. And, for a long time now, people have believed that Genesis chapter one was the story of creation. However, we now find out that it is only a story of *re-creation*, and that actually the story of *original* creation is Genesis chapter two and three—the Eden account.

The Bible has been correct all along. The Bible states that the Earth is round (Isaiah 40:22). The Bible also states that Eden is the original creation account (Gen. 2:4–3:24; Job 38:4–7; Ps. 51:5; John 3:18; Romans 1:21, 3:23; Eph. 1:4–5, 11). But, we just didn't get it.

Even so, paradigms are hard to change. Back in history, when the Earth was *known* to be flat, there were only a few who thought it to be round. And today, even though it is accepted by most that the priests who put the Hebrew scrolls of the Torah of Moses, and the creation accounts together (during the time of David) got it right, there have always been some who thought that the two creation accounts didn't quite fit. When we recognize that God speaks in riddles and parables (Matt. 13:9–17; 17–20), we can understand that it doesn't matter which creation event we read first in Scripture, because the truth lies in reading all Scripture—piecing all the puzzle pieces together to truly see the full picture.

Today, there are two sets of understanding concerning origins. Let us analyze which is the creation story of *origin*, and which is the story of *re*-creation, and how resolving this puzzle actually solves many other puzzles, including *predestination*.

Studying God's Word is like putting together a 10,000-piece puzzle. And, this puzzle of God's Word is a difficult one, where all the pieces are the same basic color. God's Word is like a puzzle of great light, and the entire picture is a great white light, and each piece is a piece of that light—the same white color on every piece. The only difference between each piece is its shape, its unique fit, and its proportion—its unique truth.

If you've ever participated with others in piecing together a puzzle, you know it starts out fairly easy. The pieces on the outside (the border), go together pretty quickly. Then, it gets really difficult to fit different pieces together, especially where they are all the same color. With different people all trying to fit the pieces together, sooner or later, someone finds a piece which seems so close to fitting that they press it a little to force it into place. Later on, what usually happens is that there are lots of other pieces and sections of the picture that just don't seem to fit together anywhere. Then, someone finds that this one little piece was forced into place by someone awhile back. It actually doesn't really fit into that place, even though it seemed right at the time, and even though everyone accepted that it belonged there all this time (because that is where it was found). But now, with more pieces assembled, it becomes clear that this piece, which everyone assumed belonged there, doesn't actually fit there. It belongs in a different place. But, we must note that just as it required a little force to put this piece into the *wrong* place, it will now require force to remove it. There will be resistance.

Assembling the Scripture puzzle takes time. Thousands of attempts are made to try and fit pieces together. Through all the attempts to fit pieces together, every now and then we may discover that a piece that we all accepted as orthodox (because it has always been interpreted as fitting that way), now has a slightly different fit. This is not the fault of the puzzle (God's Word). This is not the fault of God—God and His Word are a perfect fit. This is a human problem. We are limited. We are not God; therefore, we are not able to see how all the pieces truly fit together. That is, until someday we are able to completely assemble God's Word. One day, when these pieces are finally matched up (so that all the pieces fit together comfortably and agree with one another), then we will have a complete picture of God's light, His wisdom, His plan. Unfortunately, this may not occur during our lifetime. The puzzle is still being put together. Satan is constantly disrupting our understanding.

There are many puzzle pieces within God's Word, which we humans have not yet fully comprehended. Subjects such as:

Puzzle Piece #1: Are *the creation accounts* of Genesis 1, and Genesis 2 and 3, two accounts of the *same* creation event, or two accounts of two *different* creation events? And, if these are two separate creation events (the Hebrew/early Christian position), then, which came first? Have past generations of scholars forced this piece into a wrong place where it only "seems" to fit?

Puzzle Piece #2: How does God's sovereignty, and our free will, fit together with God's predestination? This puzzle piece of predestination, scholars can't seem to fit anywhere. (see section on *Predestination*).

Puzzle Piece #3: Is sin inherited in some way from Adam and Eve? Or, are we each personally responsible for sin, even in the womb, before we are even born? Are babies innocent, or guilty of sin? Have we really found the correct fit for this puzzle piece of Original Sin? (see section on *Original Sin*)

Puzzle Piece #4: There are many views of the *millennium*. There are many ways scholars are trying to fit this puzzle piece of God's Word into the picture. Where does it really fit? [33, 66, 67]

The puzzle of God's Word is an ongoing project. The puzzle is not complete. The entire picture is not yet clear. Others before us have placed what pieces we do have into place. Perhaps a couple of pieces are actually misplaced. God's Word is correct, the pieces do fit somewhere, but perhaps a couple of pieces have been forced into a place they truly don't fit. This means that, today, when we begin to try and fit in new pieces, having accepted the puzzle as correct the way we received it, we find many pieces which don't quite fit. Perhaps, more pieces could fit, if we could find the piece, or pieces, which have been forced into place in the past.

A good example of a simple thing we have in our Bibles today, which everyone accepts at first (because it's the way we received it), are the divisions of chapters and verses. For example, Genesis chapter 1 ends in verse 31, and then chapter 2 begins. At first, the assumption is that chapter one is a set of common thoughts, and chapter two begins a new thought. However, the original Hebrew, Arabic, and Greek, have no such divisions. These were added later as the Bible was translated into English. And, in fact, all scholars today (including the Hebrew scholars), agree that Genesis chapter 1 actually ends at Genesis 2:3, and that Genesis chapter 2 actually begins at Genesis 2:4. The first three verses of Genesis chapter two are a summary conclusion for chapter one, and don't really belong in chapter 2.

In this book, we will discover the old Hebrew rabbinical understanding of the Old Testament texts, and the Jewish Greek understandings of both the Old and New Testament texts, and compare these understandings with current evidence, as well as pieces of the puzzle of God's Word, which have been assembled since the time of Christ, always using Scripture to test Scripture. By doing this, we will try and determine if certain puzzle pieces actually belong where someone in the past has put them.

For example, should Genesis chapter 1 come ahead of Genesis chapters 2 and 3? Let us explore some Hebrew understandings of Genesis, and see if perhaps these pieces fit comfortably in another arrangement. Whereas, the way they are arranged now seems a little forced [33].

Because God speaks to us in puzzles or parables, it seems clear that Moses received the creation narratives exactly as we have them recorded today, and that God's intention is for us to search the Scriptures to discover exactly which creation event comes first, and thereby understand our real need for reconciliation and redemption—our real need for a Savior. God gives us all the evidence we need right in the Scriptures.

Even so, many scholars suggest that the oral stories, or written Hebrew scrolls of the Torah (including the two creation account narratives), which were all handed down from Moses, were compiled by various sources during the period of David (around 1000 BC). The sources for these writings have been attributed to *J*, *E*, *D*, and *P* sources. The *J* and *E* sources are the oldest, *J* referring to *Yahweh*, the name of God used in the writings of Eden (the Germans use the letter *J*, in place of *Y* for Yahweh), and *E* referring to *Elohim*, the name of God used in writings of the 7-day creation. This is based upon many studies, and there is a good discussion of whether to accept these descriptions, or not, as well as their arrangements, and their dates, in Professor Rendsburg's work on the book of Genesis.[1]

It has been found that the Hebrew Torah contains no later-period Persian influence on the words used in the Torah, which one does find in writings done after 586 BC (the Babylonian exile). Therefore, the Torah (which includes Genesis), does, in fact, pre-date David's time.[1, 8, 9, 12] There are some who date the work of the scribe, or priest (who put the writings together), to as late as 920 BC, due to the Genesis 47:11 reference to the *land of Rameses*.

This was a reference by the scribe, or priest, to inform the readers of exactly where Israel lived in Egypt (the delta region where the city of Rameses was built). Most Egyptologists place the date of Rameses to 1250 BC, but some place the date as late as 920 BC, based upon a developing new chronology.[2] Either way, the date of the written Torah can be placed during the period of David and Solomon (1000 BC). We understand, of course, that these scrolls, and oral stories, trace all the way back to Moses, per Jesus (John 5:45–47).

Dr. William Cooper, British historian, notes that if Genesis were written during, or after, the captivity of the Israelites in Babylon (sixth and fifth centuries BC), they would have used the Babylonian and Persian calendar calculations (month and days), which the Jewish people used in all other daily life functions. However, when the days and months are written about in Genesis, exact thirty-day months are referenced (five months of 150 days— Gen. 7:11–8:4).

During and after the Jewish people were in Babylon, they used the existing knowledge of days and months, which required twenty-nine days and other adjustments, which they still use, even today. Genesis, however, is very specific as to thirty days, which agrees with the monthly patterns (which would have been in existence *before* the massive breakup of Earth, due to the flood) and further Earth-splitting (which science agrees occurred in the past such as Pangaea—the one land mass), breaking up into the continents we observe today. The Earth/

moon cycle has changed in the past (as noted in the "Age & Geology" section of the book *"Science, Origins, & Ancient Civilizations—Scientific Evidence Withheld from School Textbooks."*[65]

The original Genesis scrolls, therefore, pre-date the period of David and Solomon (1000 BC), no matter whether one's view is that the writings are directly attributed to Moses, or whether one's view is that various priests (*J, E, D,* and *P*), may have written the accounts from oral transmissions from Moses. For example, Abraham's marriage to his half-sister (1900 BC) was prohibited under Mosaic Law (Gen. 20:12; Lev. 18:9). It is *very unlikely* that the Jews of the exilic period (500 BC) would have fabricated offensive events, or preserved such stories, unless these were already part of God's record to preserve. Also, the prevalent use of the *El* compounds for the name of God (God Almighty—El Shaddai—Gen. 17:1) contrasts with their virtual absence in the first-millennium texts (1000 BC) which came later.

If one accepts the understanding that the priests assembled various scrolls to give us the biblical text we have today, then it would seem that the Hebrew scribe or priest obviously had a paradigm of the cosmos preceding the earth, and therefore, *introduces* the more cosmic event (the 7-day account), *before* the more earthly event (the Eden account). The scribe, or priest, who put the scrolls together, would have had the responsibility of keeping the exact words from the scrolls intact, and at the same time, providing *clarification* (such as in Gen. 47:11).

GENESIS 47:11
Clarification:
Genesis 47:11 is a clarification from the scribe (or priest)—simply *clarifying* for the reader (informing later generations), exactly where, in Egypt, that Israel lived (which, today, archeologists have also identified as the delta region in the area of the city of Rameses).

The question we will analyze in the following verse-by-verse study is not whether God's Word is correct and true. The words passed down from Moses are absolutely correct and true, per Jesus (John 5:45–47). The question is how we are to understand these two creation accounts when they seem so obviously different.

God's overall message in the Bible is that we are, we hope, heading to the ultimate perfect eternity, Paradise. Unfortunately, some will be forever condemned to hell. We also know that God's original creation was a perfect creation (Paradise or Eden), not the cosmic universe we see today, which science informs us is slowly dying and heading to destruction. Therefore, the original creation account of origins should be the Eden account, God's perfect creation, which is in agreement with Paradise to come (Rev. 21–22).

Eden is the account we should first read, so that we can clearly understand exactly *why we need* the 7-day re-creation event (this dying cosmos), which is a *temporary* period of time for salvation—a creation in which we find ourselves looking forward to that future time of restoration *back* to Paradise and *reconciliation* with God, for all those who trust in Christ (John 14:6). But, God speaks to us in riddles and parables (Matt. 13:9–17, 17:20), and for this reason, God gave Moses the creation narratives in a reverse order, to challenge us. But, God also gave us ample reason to question their order, because the contents and order of events of the two creation narratives are so different.

So, let us look at these two Genesis accounts. All scholars agree that Genesis 1:1 is the overall *introduction* of the original creation. This verse is written in the perfect tense, indicating that the creation work of verse one is complete. One needs to proceed to Genesis chapters 2 and 3 for the actual story of that original creation (Paradise or Eden). It is in this creation of Paradise that Satan, and then many of the host, chose the lesser good (self), over the greater good (God). And, because of this sin (pride and disobedience of God), the resulting 7-day recreation event is necessary (for a limited time), to establish God's plan of salvation (the reconciliation), the restoration of those who have sinned *back* to a relationship with God—*back* into Paradise again (Rev. 21–22).

CHAPTER 2

GENESIS CHRONOLOGY - EDEN FIRST

GENESIS 1:1
Creation of Heaven and Earth:
"In the beginning, God created the heaven (singular)*, and the earth.*

I n the ancient Hebrew text, there is also the *"alpha and tau,"* (the beginning and the end), after the word *God*. The writer of chapter one (the 7-day account), uses the word *Elohim* for God (power, creator, majesty), to describe the creation; whereas, the writer of chapters two and three (Eden), uses *Yahweh* for God (Lord God—Yhovah/Jehovah Elohim—self-existent, moral, righteous judge) in the description of original creation—Paradise. Two different Hebrew scrolls; two different names; two different events.

The word for *create* (used here in Genesis 1:1), is *bara*. In Hebrew, it means original creation, which is a different Hebrew word from create or made *asah*, which is mostly used in the 7-day creation narrative, which means re-made out of already existing material. In the original creation, *bara*, the Eden account, God is intimately involved—forming, building, planting. In the *re*-creation, *asah*, the 7-day account, God speaks as one remotely involved—distant, commanding.

Here, in this very first verse (the introduction), is the reference, not only to the original (*bara*) creation of the heaven (heaven in the Hebrew is singular) and earth, but this creation event also includes the creation of *everything*, including *all* souls, in Eden (Gen. 2:1, 4; Deut. 4:19; Neh. 9:6; Job 38:4–7; Ps. 139:16, 148:4; Jer. 1:5; Ezek. 28:13–16; Ezek. 31; Luke 3:38; John 1:11—13, 3:13, 17:5–6; Romans 8:16, 19–21, 29–30, 11:2; Gal. 4:6; Eph. 1:4–5, 11; Rev. 12:1–4). In

Genesis 2:1, the Hebrew word for host (*tsaba*) means persons, beings, angels, a mass, an army, a band, an array (see the Angels & Humans section).

There is no mention of date or time in Genesis 1:1.

Hebrew language scholars state that verse 1 is written in the perfect tense, to indicate that this work of creation in verse 1, is complete (earth formed, not formless). We must look to either Eden, or to the 7-day account to read what happened in the creation event of verse 1. Genesis 1:2 will lead us to go to Eden, because this verse 2 states that the earth was formless (*tohu wabohu*), and we know from Isaiah 45:18 that God did not create the earth formless. Therefore, Eden follows the introduction of Genesis 1:1. God speaks in parables to challenge us (Matt. 13:9–17, 17:20)

- This original creation is a different age from the one in which we are now living. Eden is an age before this age (supernatural—eternal), just as the new heaven and earth to come are yet another age in the future (1 Cor. 2:7; Heb. 1:2, 11:3; Rev. 21:1). The Jewish Talmud, including the Jewish Mishnah, teaches that Paradise (Eden) and hell, were created *before* this world (age) we live in now. In addition, they teach the pre-existence of all souls, and the righteous, being in Paradise *before* this age in which we now live.[3] *Early* Christians, such as Augustine, wrote that man was not a child of this world until he sinned[4] The early Christian understanding was that the host of heaven were created *before* the foundation of the earth was laid, Job 38:1–18.[4] The context of Job 38 is to the *re*-creation of the earth. The angels witnessed the Earth being remade/laid. *Laid* in the Hebrew implies a *change*, and these verses include *darkness* and *death*. Job 38 is *not* pointing to the original creation (*not* Eden). Job 38 is viewing the *re*-creation, the 7-day event—our temporary age of grace and reconciliation.

- Original creation: Science theorizes that an event called the "Big Bang" took place; however, the heaven and earth originally created are like the new heaven and earth to come (Rev. 21–22). They are *super*natural in nature—not natural as we experience in this age of reconciliation and grace. The Big Bang event (the natural explanation from science), could be used to describe the 7-day narrative we experience in this life today, which is more properly described as the *re*-creation event, brought on by God *after* the fall in Eden. Even so, all science agrees that at the very beginning of the Big Bang the laws of physics were suspended (supernatural).

Science theorizes that this age we are living in now formed as follows: Our universe we see today, originated out of nothing tangible. Matter existed in the form of energy. Einstein theorized, and science has since shown, that energy can become matter. As energy consolidates, it reaches a critical mass. The forces are pulling so strong that it is like a black hole, where even light energy cannot escape. When critical mass occurs, then energy explodes and a hyper-inflation (or stretching), takes place. Energy blows right through the event horizon, and, in effect, becomes a white hole, from which light escapes. The event horizon is that point where the pull of gravity is not so strong as to pull light back. Light can escape past the point of the horizon. As matter escapes, the event horizon shrinks inward.

The energy from this event includes extremely high-frequency energy—much higher than the frequency spectrum of light. The universe does the bulk of its expansion in the very first second of this expansion, or stretching event. (God's Word describes this stretching in Isa. 40:22, 42:5, 45:12, 51:13; Jer. 10:12). As this hyper-frequency energy is stretched and slows, it stabilizes within the frequency spectrum of visible light, creating a path of light from all points of the newly forming matter, thus, giving the appearance of light, billions of years old. Evidence compiled over the past couple of decades, and presented to the Physics Conference at Warwick University in 2005, shows how the speed of light has been slowing down from the creation event (Big Bang), even though science has always assumed that the speed of light is a constant.[38, 39, 65]

As this energy slows and cools, it becomes matter, just as Einstein theorized, where matter and energy are interchangeable. Matter is then consolidated by electromagnetic forces, which science measures as 10 to the power of 40 times *more powerful than gravity* in space. With forces this great, the mathematical calculations show the universe we see today could have originated in a matter of *hours*, not even requiring a whole day.[65]

Light could have also been made at the same time God created the universe, thus, giving the appearance of light billions of years old. Light, in deep space travels faster than light close to Earth, when measured with a time reference to the gravity of Earth. This effect is called "Gravitational Time Dilation." This time dilation gives the *appearance* of light billions of years old, but indicates the universe is actually very young. This effect of time dilation has been tested by scientific experiments conducted by J. C. Hafele and Richard Keating, using cesium clocks, which proved Einstein's theory. Both Dr. Gerald Schroeder, and Dr. Russell Humphreys have shown that six days of time on Earth, with its gravity, are *equal to* billions of years of time in space, which has almost no gravity.[6, 7, 65] Thus, time and age are relative to the point in space from which they are measured.

Cambridge University particle physicist John Polkinghorne, along with Nobel Laureate and Cambridge University theoretical physicist Abdus Salam, Nobel Prize-winning physicist Brian Josephson, Nobel Laureate Murray Gell-Mann (whose research led to the discovery of the Quark), and physicist Bob Russell, at a series of conferences at Oxford University, have raised serious questions as to whether an intelligent designer may be the only explanation for the unexplained aspects of physics today. Polkinghorne states, *"Physics asks how the world works, and when it answers that question it finds a very deep, marvelously patterned order. But, it doesn't explain where that order comes from."*

Examples of the unexplainable in physics include the mysteries of the uncertainty principle at the subatomic level with regards to quantum physics, as well as the mystery of chaos theory to explain large-scale events (the cosmos). Einstein was the first to show that time is not absolute. There is no universal clock, which means science cannot identify what mechanism is controlling events in our space/time continuum. Quantum physicist Antoine Suarez states, "There is no story that can be told that can explain how these quantum correlations keep occurring . . . you could say the experiments show that space time does not contain all the intelligent entities acting in the world, because something outside of time is coordinating the photons' results…there is strong experimental evidence for accepting that non-material beings act in the world."[65]

Perhaps God?

Note that in the *proper chronology* of God's creation, we now move from this introduction stating that the creation event is done (perfect tense Genesis 1:1—*bara*), to the description of God creating Paradise/Eden (*bara*). This Eden creation account begins in Genesis 2:4, and concludes at the end of Genesis chapter 3, with the fall of mankind, and our being separated from God and Paradise. The 7-day creation event is the result of the fall, which occurred during the Eden creation event. Therefore, the Eden creation event must have occurred first.

GENESIS 2:4–2:25

The Original Creation Event—Eden

Genesis 2:4 describes Adam (actually et-adam—mankind), and Eve (womankind), as being created at the beginning.

The story of creation should now move from the introduction (Genesis 1:1), to the story of Eden (Gen. 2:4ff), which was the original creation. Refer to the discussion on Genesis 1:2 (just before the 7-day account is discussed in this book), for further discussion on why Genesis 1:1 is separate from Genesis 1:2.

This Eden narrative should actually follow the Genesis 1:1 introduction (as I've placed it here), because this is where God begins, with *Paradise*. This agrees with the Hebrew understanding in the Talmud, including the Mishnah. Ultimately, Eden is where God is going to return those who are reconciled— those born again (John 3:1–7)—to *Paradise* (Rev. 21–22).

Note that God's Word actually takes us from Genesis 1:1 (original creation), and now tells us what took place *in* that original creation. Only *after* the fall of Satan, and all those Satan deceives, does God's Word then refer to the change and dissolution of that age of the perfect creation (Gen. 1:2—*tohu wabohu*—Isaiah 45:18). After the fall, we read of the *reforming* of His creation in the 7-day re-creation period, in order to accomplish His plan of *reconciliation* (Gen. 1:2–2:3; Job 38).

Genesis 2:5: The earth in Eden is *not* "formless" (Isaiah 45:18), whereas, the beginning of the 7-day narrative refers to a formless mass of waters (Gen. 1:2–8—Days 1 and 2). Eden *must* be the original creation.

There is no man to *till*, or (as the Hebrew word *abad* is translated), to *serve* the earth. In other words, there is no one that serves or worships worldly things. The heavenly host are to worship only God.

Genesis 2:6: Note that God tells us there is no rain yet, and that He causes a mist to water the earth (not rain—only a water vapor canopy).

Adam and Eve (mankind and womankind), are created here in original creation in Paradise/Eden. Note, that Adam and Eve are created separately in this original creation account, unlike the *re*-creation account of the 7-days (Gen. 1:26–28). In Revelation 4:11, we are informed that we were created for God's pleasure. Adam and Eve are generic terms for mankind and womankind in the creation accounts, and do not actually refer to particular individuals, but just to mankind and womankind.[16, 34]

The first definitive use of the word *Adam* to refer to a particular person is actually in Genesis 4:1, where the generations of this flesh age are listed. The Hebrew words are *adam* and *chavvah* (eve), and they simply mean mankind and womankind (bearer of life). There could have been many men and women.[16, 34]

Note that Isaiah 45:12 states that *flesh and blood* humans were created new (*bara*), on Day 6 at the time when earth was remade (*asah*). Mankind and womankind are created supernaturally in Eden, *not* natural flesh and blood like the 7-day account.

Plants, animals, and fowl are created for Eden. *No* water life is mentioned, and no sun is mentioned. Note that the original creation is just like the new heaven and earth in Revelation 21, where there is *no* sea (Rev. 21:1), and *no* sun, as God is light (Rev. 21:23, 22:5). The sun, moon, and stars are created in the beginning (Gen. 1:1; Rev. 12:1–2,[66] and are re-made (*asah*) on Day 4 of the 7-day creation to give light. There is no mention of plant seeds as in the 7-day narrative. Fowl in this Eden account are not identified as winged, as they are in the 7-day account. These are two separate distinct accounts of God's creative abilities.

Genesis 2:7: Mankind was created *before* the plants and animals in this Eden creation narrative. Note that adam (mankind), is created in this creation event before eve (womankind—the bearer of life), but in the 7-day event, mankind and womankind are created at the same time, on Day 6—and they are created in the 7-day *event after* the earth had been planted with trees, herbs, and grass, on Day 3.

The breath of life, spirit, and soul. Mankind is created in Eden/Paradise, in his supernatural material body, in *the image of God* (Gen. 1:27; 1 Thess. 5:23). The combination of the body and the breath of life (or spirit), come together to make one a living being (a living soul). In the Hebrew understanding, a person *is* a soul, and in the Western/Greek understanding, a person *has* a soul—two different understandings (see discussion on Spirit & Soul, in the *Final States* study or books.[66, 67] Mankind in Eden are "formed" (pinched, pressed, and molded), out of the ground like a potter with clay (lovingly forming us). Then, God breathed into us our spirit (our unique individual spiritual nature).

Note that Job and Elihu were also formed out of clay and given the breath of life, indicating their original creation in Eden prior to their flesh birth (Job 10:9, 33:4–6).

Genesis 2:8–9: Every tree. Note that God *first* plants a garden in Eden, and *then* forms these trees out of the ground (just like mankind). These trees are different trees from the regular fruit trees of the 7-day creation period of Genesis 1:11–12. For the *early* Christian, the trees in Eden represented the host of creation (pleasant to sight), as well as regular trees (good for food—see the *early* Christian position in the study *Early Christian Doctrines* or see the chapter on Angels and Humans). Today, we may find this symbolism of the tree being related to beings, to be strange. But, Jesus Himself used this imagery (Matt. 7:17–20), and about one-third of the usage of trees in God's Word actually refer to people (Mark 8:22–25). The trees created here are symbolic of the heavenly host, as well as trees for food. Note that they are referred to as pleasant and good, desirable, (not barren and dry, and casting no shade or shadow, Ezek. 31). These trees are good for their fruit (Matt. 7:17–20; Jude 11–12). Other trees are referred to here and in Genesis 2:16–17. There is also the Tree of Life, and the Tree of Knowledge of Good and Evil (which are dimensions of God), and the source of Satan's knowledge (Ezek. 31), the serpent, or shining one. God and all of His creation are represented here in Paradise (Heb. 12:22–24).

Dietrich Bonhoeffer said of the tree of life, that it was in the middle of Eden, indicating it should be the center of our focus—that God is not at the boundaries of life restricting our abilities—not limiting us—but, actually freeing us to be all that we can be—unlimited, with God at the center.

This was the first prophesy that God, the Tree of Life, would take a flesh form, make Himself a *tree*, and become like the created beings, the *trees* of creation, so as to be sacrificed as a *tree* upon a tree, for the sins of the *trees* (Judges 9; Hosea 14; Heb. 6; Ezek. 31, 47; Matt. 3:10, 7:17–2; Mark 8:24; John 6:35, 41, 48, 51, 58; Gal. 3:13; Rev. 2:7, 9:4, 22:2). Note that the trees (including the tree of knowledge of evil), are placed toward the east of Eden, east being symbolically the direction of moving away from God throughout Scripture (Gen. 11:2).

Because Genesis 2:1 states that *all* the host of *both* heaven and earth are complete, these trees must represent the host of creation, including Adam, Eve, Job, and Elihu among billions of others (Job 10:9, 33:4–6; Ezek. 31).

TREE/TREES (FOREST/FORESTS) BEINGS

Genesis 1:11—Fruit tree: Fruit with seed in it—not man.

1:12—Fruit tree: fruit with seed in it—not man.

1:29—Fruit tree: fruit with seed in it—not man.

2:9—Every tree: Some for food/some pleasant to see/one for life/one for knowledge—fruit/man—trees also from dirt.

2:16—Every tree is okay. to eat/partake of—Tree of Life also.

2:17—However, do not partake of the Tree of Knowledge.

2:24—Keep the Way of the Tree of Life.

3:8—Adam and Eve hid amongst the trees.

Deut. 12:2—Destroy evil under the trees.

20:20—Only cut trees which bear NO fruit.

Numbers 33:9—70 trees—70 nations from Noah (70 bulls sacrificed).

Exodus 15:27—70 trees—70 nations from Noah (70 bulls sacrificed).

Leviticus 23:40–42—Four types of trees—Feast of Tabernacles (Jewish tradition relates four types of trees to people).

Nehemiah 8:15—Four types of trees—Feast of Tabernacles (tradition of four types of people).

Judges 9:8–15—The trees select a king/but various trees decline/a bramble is selected.

1 Kings 4:33—Solomon spoke of trees (people), and also of beasts, birds, creeping things, and fish.

1 Chronicles 16:33—Trees will cry when God comes to judge.

Job 14:7–14—Man will die and live again, like the tree which is cut down and lives again.

Psalm 1—Righteous man like the tree living by water—never withers

37:35—Wicked spreads himself like a great bay tree—which died.

52:8—Be like the olive tree—trust in God forever.

92:12–14—Righteous will flourish like trees in the house of God.

96:12—Trees will rejoice before the Lord.

148:9—Fruitful trees and cedars will praise God.

Proverbs 3:18–19—The Tree of Life is Wisdom (understanding).

11:30—The fruit of the righteous is a Tree of Life—verse 31, we are barely saved.

Ecclesiastes 11:3—When a tree falls in the north or the south, there it shall stay (heaven or hell).

12:5—Like the almond tree—when we are old and go to our eternal home.

Song of Songs 2:3—The tree is like my son—his fruit is sweet (Gen. 2:9, 2:16).

Isaiah 6:13—The elect of Israel are like the stump of the tree.

10:18–19—The trees will be destroyed—both body and soul—only a remnant left.

14:8—The trees rejoice at the enemies being destroyed.

44:23—They praise God—mountains (nations), forests (tribes), trees (individuals).

55:12–13—The mountains (nations) sing and the trees (individuals) clap their hands—the good tree in place of a bad thorn.

56:3—If you are in the Lord, you cannot be a dry tree—even if you are ridiculed here on earth.

61:3—The plantings of God are to be called the Trees of Righteousness.

Jeremiah 11:16—God once called you a fair tree with good fruit (Gen. 2:9, 16), but now He will set fire to you.

11:19—They plotted to destroy Jeremiah, the tree with good fruit.

17:7–8—Blessed is the man who trusts the Lord—he is a tree planted by living water.

Ezekiel 17:24—All trees (people), will know how great God is.

20:45–49—Speak against the trees and the forest of the south (opposite heaven in the north).

31:3–18—Trees in Eden (Gen. 2).

47:7–12—Trees in the millennium—fed by living water—purpose to give life—verse 22, all nations will inherit Israel's covenant with God.

Daniel 4—This tree is Nebuchadnezzar.

Joel 1:12—Just as men, various trees are withered.

Zechariah 4:3–14 2—olive trees—verse 14, the two anointed ones, Joshua and Zerubbabel.

11:1–3—Various trees (people) are destroyed.

Matthew 3:10—Trees that don't bear good fruit will be destroyed in the fi3:.

7:17–18—Good trees, good fruit—Evil trees, evil fruit.

12:33—Good trees, good fruit—Evil trees, evil fruit.

Mark 8:24—I see men as trees.

Luke 3:9—Trees that don't bear good fruit will be destroyed in the fire:.

6:43–44—Good trees, good fruit—Evil trees, evil fruit.

21:29—The fig tree (Israel), and all the trees (other nations).

23:31—If they do this when "The Tree" is alive, what will they do when He is not here physically?

Romans 11:17–24—We are part of The Tree.

Jude 12—Trees with no fruit are trees twice dead—they suffer the second death.

Revelation 2:7—The Tree of Life.

7:1—The four winds are held back from the earth, the sea, and the trees.

7:3—Don't hurt the trees.

8:7—One-third of the trees are destroyed.

9:4—Don't hurt the trees, but only those men which are evil.

11:4—Two olive trees – two to testify and be resurrected (Zechariah 4:3–14).

22:2—The Tree of Life.

22:14—The Tree of Life.

In antiquity, the tree was a useful reference to the heavenly host, and those of prominence and importance. Trees represented people, and were worshipped as sources of knowledge and fertility. Jerome is quoted as writing, "We are all planted in the garden as trees."[4]

The tree holds an ancient meaning for the Jewish people. The oldest holy day for the Jewish people is Tu B'Shvat (known as the New Year for Trees, or the *revival* of trees). This holy day dates back thousands of years, and *the original purpose of this day is no longer known.* The ancient farmers believed that at this time of year (mid-January to mid-February) the sap began to flow in the fruit trees, nature was revived, and the almond tree would bud.

Different trees represent different characteristics of mankind in the Jewish tradition. Some Jewish families plant a cedar tree for a new baby boy, and a cypress tree for a new baby girl.

The Hebrew Kabbalists have an image that represents the various dynamic aspects of God, and this image is a Tree of Life with its roots in heaven, and its branches with various fruits extending to the earth. In the sixteenth century, a special dinner (Seder) was established to commemorate this day, and it is celebrated at nightfall, to symbolize human life beginning in the darkness of the womb. The Hebrews say that we were created with thirty-two teeth to represent the name of God (Elohim) being recorded thirty-two times in the story of creation. Therefore, partaking of the fruits of different trees on earth, is equivalent to partaking of the various aspects of God represented by the "Tree of Life".[69]

This holy day was also used to establish the age of trees for the purpose of sacrificial giving (Lev. 19:21–25). Since 1948, and the establishment of the new Israel, this day is now celebrated by the planting of trees, and symbolizes the concern for preservation of nature and the environment.

In the centuries after Jesus rose from death, mankind came to understand that the earth isn't flat, and that the sun doesn't revolve around the earth (the Bible was correct all the time). As a result, around the fourth century, it became important for men of education not to appear influenced by anything which seemed too mythical. During these later centuries, (because of the influence of the Greek understanding), the understanding of the trees of creation (Gen. 2:9) changed, from being the representation of the host of Eden (Ezek. 31)—to being natural trees. The "sons of God" (Gen. 6) changed from being fallen angels—to being natural children of Seth. The angels (with supernatural bodies), became spirits with no bodies (the body being evil and meaningless to the Greeks because only the spirit lives on), thus firmly separating mankind from angels. This led to the early practice of flogging the body, or punishing the body (like Martin Luther did), as a way of striking evil.

Genesis 2:7, 2:9: "Trees" were "formed" out of the ground (clay), just as was mankind/et-adam (Job 10:9, 33:4–6—pressed and squeezed out of clay). God tells us that the stars (or angels) of heaven were called "sons of God" (Job 38:1–7). God also tells us that Adam was a son of God (Luke 3:38—supernatural in Eden). God also tells us that we, who are "born again" (John 3:1–7), will become sons of God (like the angels—Matt. 22:30; Mark 12:25; Luke 20:35–36; 1 Cor.

15:49), reconciled *back* to God after the fall (Ezek. 47:21–23; John 1:12–13; Romans 5:10–11, 8:14, 19; 2 Peter 1:4; 1 John 3:1–2; Rev. 12:1–4; Deut. 32:7–8, (v. 8, in the Septuagint reads *ben-el*—"angels of God," not "sons of Israel"—the fallen host of heaven have become the various nations of the world).

Genesis 2:10–14: "Tigris and Euphrates." These are names given by God for rivers *in Eden*, and names *later applied in this age* to rivers common to the Mesopotamian area, where Noah settled *after* the flood.

Genesis 2:15: Man is formed in this original creation period to tend to Paradise, *not* to subdue and replenish the earth, as those created on Day 6 of the 7-day creation period (Gen. 1:28). Two different functions. The 7-day creation period has a different purpose.

Eve is "made," denoting a personal involvement of God. Whereas, in the Genesis one account (7-day), both man and woman are "made/created" for the age of redemption/reconciliation, *after* the fall. They were "made/created" in the 7-day account by a distant involvement of God (see Gen. 1:26–27).

Genesis 2:16–17: Man was warned that he would die in that "day." There are two meanings here: They would die, *spiritually*, that very day, separated from God. This is part of the early Christian beliefs, per Irenaeus [15], and further, they would die *physically*. A day equals 1,000 years (2 Pet. 3:8). Note that man lived 930 years, just under 1,000 years in the re-made earth—there is scientific evidence for long lives.[65] There was *no* death until they sinned. There was *no* death, *no* evolution, prior to Adam and Eve and the fall (Mark 10:6; Romans 8:19–23).

Blood, in this flesh age we now live in, represents the *life* of animals and man (Lev. 17:11; Deut. 12:23; Heb. 9:15–18, 22). Plants (biblically), are not part of death—only those with blood. Death (for those with blood), begins only after the fall (Romans 5:12; 1 Cor. 15:21–22)—after the re-creation events of animals and mankind with blood. All creation was cursed in the fall (Rom. 8:19–23), not just mankind (Genesis 3:14—animals; Gen. 3:17–19—thorns; Gen. 3:21—blood).

The 7-day events are single 24-hour day events—not long time periods with death and evolution prior to mankind's sin (see the 7-day creation events next, after this Eden creation event).

The Tree of Life is for supernatural beings, *not* plants and animals. Adam and Eve and the host with the "breath of life" in Eden had a *free will*. And, being creations, they need the Tree of Life, or face death/separation if they do not abide in the Tree of Life.

Genesis 2:18: Why did God say: "*It is not good for man to be alone?*" As Christians, we understand that we are to worship God with all our heart, soul, and mind (Luke 10:27). Jesus described our love and relationship with God is to be so great as to make any other relationships seem as hate (Luke 14:26). So, as Christians, we are all to experience this great relationship with God—so great a relationship, as to make any other seem unnecessary. All the host of heaven, including Adam and Eve, were created to fellowship with God. Note that the focus of the host of heaven is always upon God—not each other.

And yet, God, when He created us in perfection, in Eden, said that: "*it is not good that man* (mankind), *should be alone: I will make a help mate for him/them.*" Why, if we were created to experience this great relationship with God, in Eden, did God say that, "*it is not good,*" and further say that, "*man would be alone?*" And, why didn't God just create another similar being? Why did God find it necessary to create a being capable of giving birth, especially when, in the creation in Eden, there is no need for procreation (Gen. 2:1—the creation, and *all* beings, of *both* heaven and earth, are finished).

There was no need for procreation in Eden, yet God *foreknew* that of these created beings (the host of heaven), that *some* would fall, and this was to be His plan of reconciliation (this flesh age He created—the age we now live in), where we experience birth, and death—condemned, but given the hope of reconciliation. When one-third of the host sinned (Rev. 12:1–4), including Adam, Eve, and Satan, we separated ourselves from God, and became essentially alone—disconnected from our source of life—disconnected from the meaning of life, which is focusing upon God.

In heaven, the host (trees), don't marry each other (Luke 20:35). Therefore, all other trees (host) were unsuitable for Adam in God's plan of reconciliation, which requires babies to be born. So, God formed Eve *out of Adam*, "bone of *my* bone, flesh of *my* flesh." A specially created being to enable births.

Genesis 2:18–20: Animals created in Eden were to *complement* adam (mankind), but God foreknew that some host of heaven would deny Him, and thus, the other animals were not sufficient. This is a different creation from the 7-day, where animals were created to be *ruled* over by mankind (Gen. 1:26).

Genesis 2:21 and 23: Adam and Eve are "flesh and bone," just as Christ, after His death and resurrection, was "flesh and bone" (Luke 24:39; John

20:26–31). Note that 1 Corinthians 15:50 says that "flesh and *blood* cannot inherit heaven," meaning one must be spirit also, be "born again" (John 3:6–7). We must become spiritual beings, just as the heavenly host are supernatural beings—having an eternal nature—having a relationship with God.

Genesis 2:24–25: "Therefore"—"for this reason"—Note, the narrative does not say Adam and Eve were married—but, "for this reason" *future* generations in the flesh world to come will be "woven," and "cleave."

GENESIS 3:1–6
Satan's deception, and Adam and Eve are driven out of Paradise/Eden:

- Note that no time period is mentioned between Genesis 2:25 and 3:1.

- The serpent is an unclean animal (Lev. 11:42).

- Satan was the first to sin (Isaiah 14:12–23; Ezek. 28:11–29, Ezek. 31; Rev. 12:1–9).

The fall involves Satan, and the fallen angels, which includes mankind and womankind. Revelation 12:1–4 tells us that about the one-third of the host sinned. It is interesting that in Revelation 12:1–4 the image of the woman has twelve stars, and the dragon sweeps away one-third of the stars. Later on, some of those stars (having been cast to earth), give birth to the Messiah, Jesus (see the section on Angels & Humans). Jesus comes through Israel. Thus, the woman is seen as representative of Israel. However, the woman in heaven represents much more. The woman represents *all* the host of creation (all those "betrothed" to God), and some of these become Israel. Twelve, in Hebrew (twelve stars), represents fullness, completion (Gen 2:1). These twelve stars represent *all* the host of creation, including the one-third that sinned.[66]

Deuteronomy 32:7–8 states in the Septuagint that all the nations of the world are established by the fallen angels—the "angels of God—*ben el*— *not* the "children of Israel."

Romans 5:12 says, "*because all sinned*" (a reference to sin in *the past)*.[10, 42, 67] In Romans 5:12, sin enters this world (this age), through Adam (the first human being on the re-made planet). Yet, we know Satan sinned first. Therefore, Eden (where sin first appeared), and this age we are now in, are, in fact, different.

Sin is disobeying our Creator, and choosing the lesser good (self), over the greater good (God). References to God creating evil (such as Prov. 16:4, and Isaiah 45:7), are references to the *re*-created fallen age we are now in, not to the period in Eden—nor to the new Eden, or Paradise, yet to come (Rev. 21–22). Satan, using his free will, chose self in Eden (Ezek. 28:11–19; Ezek. 31; Isaiah 14:12–23), just as the host that have fallen also used their free will to choose self above God (Ezek. 31, Rev. 12:1–9).

Genesis 3:3: The woman believes she can't even touch the fruit. But God did not condemn anyone for touching (encountering, or coming into contact with) the tree. The sin was *partaking* of it (the knowledge of evil).

Genesis 3:6: The woman is tempted by the same three things Satan used to tempt Christ and uses to tempt us: Lust of the flesh (good for food), lust of the eyes (pleasant to the mind), and, pride of life (to make one wise)—Matt. 4; Luke 4; 1 John 2:16). The issue is either trust God and deny self, or trust in self, and define good and evil for ourselves, thus, denying God.

Genesis 3:1–6: To "eat" is to put your faith in (not to physically eat). To "eat" is to believe (trust—eat the "bread of life"—the Word—see John 1 and 6:35, 50–56). This fall of adam (mankind), and womankind, the host of heaven, and Satan's corruption of Paradise, are the source of the curse on humankind (2 Chron. 6:36; Psalm 51:5, 58:3; Romans 1:21–23, 3:23; 1 John 1:8–10, 3:8; Rev. 12:1–4).

We'll come back to Genesis 3 after we analyze the Original Sin, and then The Curse.

CHAPTER 3

ORIGINAL SIN
ITS MEANING—ITS SOURCE

Liberalism has become more pronounced within the last two hundred years, due primarily to the influence of science, and a more intellectual, self-centered world. There has been an effort to diminish God, diminish the Bible, and diminish Jesus, in order to justify our human desires, which don't agree with God's commands. But, liberalism did not begin only two hundred years ago. Liberalism, in theology (the rejection of the supernatural, the rejection of miracles, the rejection of Jesus as fully God and fully man, the rejection of the Bible as inspired by God and inerrant in the original text), has been around as long as Satan. Of course, even the existence of Satan is also rejected by many liberals. Satan's plan is working well.

Put simply, if the Bible is inspired and inerrant, the liberal has no case. Conversely, if the Bible is not inspired and errant, the fundamentalist has no case. However, the Bible has proven to be worthy to be called the inspired Word of God because of *evidence*:

The oldest authenticated sets of manuscripts of Scripture in the world are of the Bible. Jewish people, Christians, and Muslims all refer to these Scriptures.

The prophecies of the Bible (except for the end-time events) are 100 percent fulfilled, and many are *extremely detailed*. Some Christians believe we are approaching the end times now, but no one other than God knows for sure.

Archeology supports the Bible. And, in fact, the new chronology being pieced together (concerning Egyptian pharaohs and the timeline of the Bible), now show the Bible is correct all the way back as far as Egyptian records can go.[2, 67, 68]

Jesus quoted His Word (the Bible), thus giving the Bible authority. And, Jesus proved Himself to be God through miracles—His resurrection, and His ascension into heaven, with the promise to return. All this was witnessed by hundreds, and recorded in the Bible (Acts 1:1–8; 1 Cor. 15:1–8).

The liberal theologian tries to challenge the empty tomb, the resurrection accounts seen by hundreds over several weeks (Acts 1:1–8; 1 Cor. 15:1–8), and the total turnaround of the disciples—from being fearful for their lives, to being bold martyrs after the ascension. However, this weight of evidence remains to this day as un-refuted, bold testimony to the deity of Christ, our only path to salvation (John 14:6), and to the truthfulness of the Bible (John 14:6; Acts 4:12).

One truth in particular (that of *original sin* and the total depravity of man) has many understandings, none of which are adequate, because none of them, including the fundamental, seem to totally agree with Scripture.

Liberals, on the one hand, simply reject the truth that all humans are sinners. They reject God's Word. Enns, in his book *The Moody Handbook of Theology*, lists numerous pages of liberal theologians who reject original sin. We can ignore these liberal understandings because they also reject the Scriptures as inspired, and deny God as the source of the Bible.

Fundamentalists also seem to miss the message of God when this subject of the *source* of sin is interpreted. We are all sinners, *yes*. But, the genuine source of our sin is actually different from the modern fundamental understanding as well. The doctrine of original sin is that event associated with the time of Adam in Eden (Paradise), in which each of us is guilty of having rebelled against God and disobeyed.

As Millard J. Erickson states in his book *Introducing Christian Doctrine*, "There is a definite connection between Adam's sin, and all persons of all times. In some way, his sin is not just the sin of an isolated individual, but is also our sin. Because we participate in that sin, we all, from the beginning of life (perhaps even from the point of conception), receive a corrupted nature along with a consequent inherited tendency toward sin."[42]

So far, so good. But how does each person become guilty and individually responsible for this sin of Adam's time?

Some theologians suggest that each generation either *inherits* sin or has sin *imputed* (declared) upon them from Adam. Additionally, there is some disagreement amongst various fundamentalists as to whether a child is considered saved before that child's "age of accountability." In other words, a child is a sinner (supposedly because of Adam), but somehow not guilty of sin until some age of accountability. Somehow a child, even though a sinner, is saved without being *born again* (John 3:3–7). There is, however, no scriptural evidence to support these views. Passages such as 2 Samuel 12:23, and Matthew 18:3 and 19:14, fall short of saying that children are saved because of their age. Romans 7:9 is used by some to say that children are innocent until their age of accountability, meaning that when a child understands their sin, then, at that point, a child becomes subject to the condemnation of God.

However, Romans 5:12–14 states that we are all condemned to death because of our sin, even though we may not have received the law yet. Jesus actually warns us against restraining or hindering a child from accepting Him, which indicates each child *individually* must trust in Jesus, and does not imply an automatic salvation if they die young, or die due to abortion.

The source of original sin has been attributed by many theologians to various forms of imputation from Adam. It is commonly said, "As the sin of Adam is imputed to me, so also is the righteousness of Christ imputed to me." Christ's righteousness *is* declared (imputed) to each follower (Romans 4:16–25). However, there is no scriptural support for the imputation of Adam's sin to other people. Adam, by some, is defined as a representative of us all by being a federal head, or leader, thus representative of us all. Others refer to the natural headship explanation (the Traducian Theory), where we supposedly inherit our soul, as well as a physical body, from our parents. Therefore, we supposedly inherit sin through the blood, along with our flesh body, which is subject to death from Adam down through the generations.

Donald Guthrie, in *New Testament Theology*, states that, "Although Paul maintains that sin entered this world through Adam (Romans 5:12), Paul does not argue from the one (Adam), to the many (all people), as if he were heaping the responsibility of everyone's sin on Adam's head." In Paul's theology we are each individually responsible for our sin in the past (Romans 5:12).

To quote Rabbi Joseph Telushkin, "The idea that every child is born damned for the sin of Adam is alien to Jewish thought."[63]

To quote J. W. MacGorman, "Much of the misunderstanding of Romans 5:12–21 has stemmed from a translation error in the Latin Vulgate of the fourth century, where the Greek text states 'because all sinned,' was mistakenly rendered 'in whom all sinned,' with Adam regarded as the unnamed antecedent of 'in whom'."[61] And again in the seventeenth century Johannes Cocceius proposed a *theory* of God entering into a covenant with Adam as the 'federal head' of the human race. This greatly influenced the Reformation. However, there is not one shred of biblical evidence of this."

We do *inherit death*, the result of sin, but *not the sin* of Adam. Erickson describes the imputation of the righteousness of Christ as "not a matter of transferring righteousness from Him to me, as it is a matter of bringing the two of us together, so that we hold all things in common."[42] However, this is not the same philosophy of imputation that is used to describe the imputation of sin to us from Adam, which is described by many as a physical transfer as part of our fleshly birth (the Traducian Theory).

Concerning sin, Erickson writes, "It is a matter of transferring Adam's sin and sinful nature to me."[42] These various philosophies try to explain why the Bible teaches that each of us is a sinner, *even in the womb*, before we are even born—but they fall short of using actual Scripture to support these various imputation theories. Scripture points to God knowing *before* the creation of the world, *before* our birth, that all are sinners, and in need of His (Jesus') sacrifice to be saved. (Psalm 51:5, 58:3; Matt. 19:17; Acts 2:23; Eph. 1:4–5, 11; Romans 3:12, 23, 8:28–30, 9:11–16, 11:2, 7; Rev. 12:1–4).

There is no scriptural comparison of the imputing of Christ's righteousness, and the so-called imputing of Adam's sin to us. The imputing of Christ's righteousness is *not* to all. Whereas, the *supposed* imputing of sin from Adam *is* to all. All will die. But Romans 5:15 and 19 state *many*, *not all* were affected by Adam. All have sinned, but not all are saved. Concerning the concept of being joined together with Christ, the picture presented in the Bible is one of being given new clothes, of our clothes being washed, of being represented to the Godhead by Jesus as being given a right standing, of being justified, of Jesus' righteousness being placed into my account to pay off my debt, so that I am presented debt-free to the Godhead. Those who are declared righteous receive a new, material, supernatural body, but do not receive God's powers.

In the same way, we inherit our corrupt flesh physically from Adam, but *not* his sin. From Adam we are materially made flesh, and do inherit death, but *not* Adam's sin (Deut. 24:16; Ezek. 18:20). As it says in Romans 5:12, "*we all sinned*" (past tense), meaning we each are responsible for our own sin *in the past*, and therefore, all are condemned to death in this age (John 3:18). This is further confirmed in Romans 5:19, where the passage says that *many* were made sinners. This can only be true if the fall occurred in Eden (where *many* fell, but *not all*— Rev. 12:3–4). Many of the nations of this world (the fallen) will be restored (Ezek. 47:21–23; Deut. 32:7–8—v. 8 in the Septuagint reads "angels of God"— ben el, *not* "sons of Israel"—the fallen host of heaven have become the nations of this world). Romans 5:19 would have to read *all* were made sinners (if referring to this age), because all other passages tell us we are all sinners, even at conception— not one is righteous.

Because we are created in the image of God, and God is good, and God loves us, many assume babies are innocent. There is a complete disconnect between what we think about ourselves (being good), and what the Bible actually records (John 3:18; Romans 3:10–12). Babies are destined for hell. Babies are not innocent. All are sinners because all have sinned (past tense), and we are all condemned to hell at conception. Many people seeking truth are caused to reject a personal relationship with God, because God is presented today as arbitrary and unjust, when God is seen as declaring us sinners at conception, seemingly without us being somehow personally responsible for sin and, when God predestines some to eternal life in His kingdom, while others are predestined to hell. See the section on Predestination.

Today in Christianity, we don't begin with the understanding that we are all condemned to death because we are all sinners. Instead, we mistakenly begin with the understanding that God loves us, and immediately find conflict with God's Word, which says He condemns us to death from conception. If we correctly present the truths of original sin, predestination, final states, and the millennium, people would clearly understand their *personal responsibility* for their sin, and their true *need* for the sacrifice of Jesus, and God's overall plan of *reconciliation*.

More than ever, in a pluralistic society where people are seeking truth, we are confronted by Christian understandings of how we arrive at doctrines, or truths, which are not supported by Scripture. Instead, conclusions are reached by good intentions and the philosophies of man. For the person who can accept Jesus by simply hearing that God loves us, and died for us, there is no problem for them on how we arrive at our understanding of truth and doctrines. But even Christians such as this will have questions once they begin reading Scripture.

Christianity needs to evaluate its own misunderstandings of how we arrive at our conclusions. Ironically, we can accept the *conclusions* of these doctrines (the truths of original sin and predestination) in the same way as conventional, traditional, conservative Christianity. But, we understand from Scripture that *the reason* we arrive at the conclusions of these doctrines, or truths, is completely different from today's conventional Christian teaching. It is imperative that our teachings represent Scripture, and not philosophy.

From Adam we inherit a flesh body, death, and a sinful nature, but *not* the original sin we are each responsible for; just as from Christ, we do *not* inherit righteousness, rather righteousness is declared to us (or put on us) if we have faith and trust in Christ. Righteousness is deposited to our account, we are clothed in a new garment, we are adopted, we are grafted in, as a result of *God leading* some to accept Jesus as Lord and Savior.

One need not accept the supposition that we have all been imputed with the actual sin of Adam and then that God, by His sovereign will, arbitrarily selects some to be saved, and the rest to perish (as it is presented by some fundamentalists). That requires Adam's sin to be transferred to me, not of my will, but of God's decision to somehow declare us as sinners at conception in the womb. Scripture does not seem to support this. We are guilty of sin in the womb because of our own personal sin in the *past* (Rom. 5:12).[67]

The early church understood that babies were sinners and subject to eternal separation from God. In fact, the church fathers thought that baptism might save them, so they required infant baptism. Babies are not innocent, and theologians agree we all are sinners, and therefore, we sin. However, they have struggled with the exact event which makes us sinners in the first place, even as a baby, even in the womb. Many church fathers found it difficult to accept any concept of what we would call inherited guilt. To most of them, disobedience was a *personal act*, repeated in each individual, but *not* directly inherited from Adam.[4] We are *guilty* of sinning because of our own *personal decision* to disobey God, and not simply because Adam sinned. We inherit a sinful nature from Adam, as well as death, but we are *personally* guilty of sin —at conception, in the womb— because of our own *personal* action in the *past*.

Theologians basically agree that the Greek words Paul used in Romans 5:12 mean that each person, *individually*, in the *past*, turned from God. The *aorist* tense is used specifically by Paul when he says "we all sinned," pointing to a single *past* action *somehow tied* to the sin of Adam in the past.[42]

This same reference to "all have sinned" (meaning a turning from God in the past) is noted in many other passages as well (Psalm 51:5, 58:3; Ezek. 31; Jer. 1:5; John 3:18; Acts 2:23; Romans 1:20–32, 3:12, 23; 1 John 1:8–10; Rev. 12:1–4). Romans 5:12 also says that through one man (Adam), sin entered into the world (*kosmos*). Yet, we know sin existed earlier, with Satan, in Paradise (Eden), prior to anyone else sinning, and prior to *this* world (age). Adam did bring sin into "*this world*" (this creation), but Adam and Satan sinned originally in Eden/ Paradise. Scripture indicates that we did also. Romans 3:10–12 reads that *all* turned aside—*together* we have become worthless. Romans 3:23 indicates that "all have sinned"—a past action (see also Ezek.31).

In Job 10:9 and 33:4–6, note that Adam was not the only one created from clay (to be eternal in Eden), and has now become flesh. This is an indication we were all created in Eden as clay (to be eternal), and exist now in the flesh to die because of our sins.

The words "we all sinned" in Romans 5:12 are interpreted by some to mean that all mankind sinned because of their being descendants from Adam. In Joshua 7 the story is often used to explain the Jewish understanding of how one man's sin was linked to the family. One should note, however, that in Joshua 7 only *contemporaries* were included in God's judgment, not future generations. Those who were direct family members, in existence at the time of the sin, were judged, not future generations of Israel. This Jewish understanding actually agrees with the understanding of all the host of heaven who were *contemporaries* of Eve (and deceived like Eve), being the ones judged as sinners—not future generations of humans (Deut. 24:16; Ezek. 18:20).

In Romans 5:13–14, we are told that all are condemned to death because of sin (even though those generations from Adam to Moses were not guilty of sin). So, obviously, they were guilty of some sin *in the past*, as they were not guilty of sins during their lifetime (in this creation), which were listed in the law given to Moses *later*. Therefore, the sin of which they are guilty is their sin in Eden, the original creation.

The sin of Adam was trespassing (*abar*—Hosea 6:7) against the law given by God directly to Adam, not to partake of a certain tree. The sin of Eve was allowing herself to be deceived, and missing the mark (Hebrew—*chata*, Greek—*hamartano*—Romans 3:23, 5:12), or falling short. Thus, all are sinners (*chata, hamartano*), even though many did not transgress the laws of God given to Moses (Romans 5:13–14) like Adam did. Adam (a son of God) had the law. But, those born from Adam are sons of man (Luke 3:38).

The doctrine of original sin (we are all sinners at conception) is not changed by rejecting these various understandings of imputation. But, how we view the *actual source* of original sin does affect our understanding of our true relationship with God, His justice, and our *real need* for redemption and reconciliation, even at the point of conception in the womb. We are not good people who *become* sinners—we are sinners who *need* reconciliation, or we go to hell.

As Shirley Guthrie notes in her book *Christian Doctrine*, "The word "Adam" means simply "man" in Hebrew. The story of Adam is the story of every man."[34] The proper name "Adam" was not really applied to one certain person until God chose one man, a certain "Adam," to be expelled from Eden/Paradise, to the earth we now know, to begin the fleshly human age we are all in now.

In Matthew 20:28, it says that Jesus died to pay a ransom for *many* (not all). One pays a ransom to *restore back* what was *lost*, or taken. In Romans 7:14, it says that we are sold as a slave into sin. We are stuck in sin, and need the ransom paid. The question arises, if we are sold by someone *else* into the slavery of sin, how are we then responsible for our sin? In Genesis 3, we are told how, in Eden (Paradise), *we* trusted in Satan, the deceiver. Thus, *we are responsible* for our sin, because *we* made a freewill decision to go along with Satan, turning our back on God. We are responsible for our sin against God, and God has paid the ransom to *restore* those who trust in Christ *back* into that relationship with God that we once had in Eden—reconciliation (Romans 5:10–11).

In Isaiah 14:17, God's Word tells us that Satan doesn't want his prisoners (those who were deceived and have fallen), to go home (*back* to God's kingdom—Eden). We are prisoners here on earth.

Jesus, in Luke 4:18–20, tells the world that He (God in the flesh) has come to proclaim freedom to the prisoners. This piece of Scripture is a quote from Isaiah 61:1–2. Here in Luke, Jesus did not finish the quote, which is, "He has come to proclaim freedom to the prisoners . . . *and also the day of vengeance of God*" (emphasis mine). Jesus came two thousand years ago and proclaimed freedom to the prisoners, and restored many to His kingdom (reconciliation to all those who will trust their lives to Him), and Jesus will return very soon to bring justice to those who have not trusted their lives to Him.

God foreknew and predestined us *before* the foundation of the earth. This means that He planned for salvation and judgment *before* the foundation of the world. This means we were *foreknown* to Him as sinners, which means we had sinned *before* the foundation of the world (Job 38:1–18). God does tell us (Gen. 2:1), that all the host of heaven and earth were *finished* by the end of the seven-days of creation.[23] No new souls are being created today.

So, before the foundation of this earth age, God created us, we knew Him, we disobeyed Him, and God knew our hearts (whether we were ashamed, or displayed contempt—Genesis 3). Out of His love for us, He predestined a plan of redemption and reconciliation to save those whose hearts showed shame, such as Adam and Eve (Isaiah 46:9–10). Whereas, those who showed contempt, such as Satan, are destined for destruction. Therein is the source of our freewill decision concerning our love for God (or lack of it), from which God predestined us into this earth age. We either were ashamed, or showed contempt, at the fall in Eden (Gen. 3; Job 38:4, 7; Ezek. 28, 31; Romans 9:11–16; Eph. 1:4–5; Rev. 12:1–4).

Many question whether we have any relationship with "angels." When Jesus was questioned about "humans" in Luke 20:27–33, He responded by referring to angels. Jesus tells us that angels *in heaven* do not marry, and also that in the resurrection we will be *like the angels* (Luke 20:35–36; Matt. 22:30; Mark 12:25; 2 Peter 1:4). Jesus even remarks that at the judgment, those who deny Christ will be cast into the fire *prepared for the angels* (Matt. 25:41). What did the early Christians say? Gregory of Nyssa said the resurrection promises us nothing else than the restoration of the fallen to their ancient state, an angelic life. Chrysostom said man led life like the angels, until the fall. Gregory of Nazianzus tells us that man is a "new angel," meaning an angel now in a flesh body.[21, 70]

Many wonder exactly why God uses such specific details like the 153 fish harvested on the right side of the boat in John 21:3–12. I'm not into all the number-counting schemes many get into, but John was inspired by God on a couple of occasions to use very specific numbers, both in the book of John and in the Revelation. Both the Hebrew and Greek languages used letters to refer to numbers, and numbers to refer to letters. Everyone recognizes that there is a letter-to-number representation in 666, used in Revelation 13. In the Hebrew, 153 translates to *beni Ha-Elohim* (sons of God, angels), just as used in Genesis 6, where the fallen angels came to women before the flood of Noah. In the Greek, *sons of God* is also related to the number 153, translating to 3 x 7 x 153, which means, the perfection of God's purpose is in the sons of God. John Trench, in his *Notes on the Miracles of Our Lord,* noted that this "definite number, even as the number of the elect, is fixed and pre-ordained . . . being equal to the angels." Augustine referred to the 153 as symbolically representing the saved. Jerome referred to the 153 as the elect gathered into the kingdom of God.

Here in John, the *beni Ha-Elohim* are not the fallen angels who are condemned by God (Jude 6), but are the *beni Ha-Elohim* who are reconciled and saved (Rom. 5:10–12). God's precise use of 153 to describe the fish harvested into His kingdom on the right side of the boat is to inform us that we have fallen (just like Adam and Eve fell). And, just as Adam and Eve were banished to the earth to die as humans, we also will die, having been born as flesh humans. Yet, God will save all those who trust in Him (John 3:1–7)—the perfection of God's purpose—the reconciliation of the sons of God.

The picture of the host being with the Creator prior to the fall (the separation from God) is given by Jesus in the parables in Luke 15. Note that all the sheep, all the coins, and both sons were with the owner (father), *before* they were *lost.* God gave one son (in the third parable) his free will when he gave the son his portion of the estate (in the Middle Eastern culture this parable would have violated the Jewish law, and been seen as a sin, because the son must respect the father and never seek the inheritance before the father's death). The son freely chose to separate himself from the father (just as Adam and Eve and one-third of the host chose to follow Satan). Then, while in a foreign land and facing death, he sought forgiveness, humbled himself, returned to be reconciled, and found salvation with the father (just as today, we can humble ourselves and be reconciled back to God). Note that the brother (symbolically, the host of heaven who remained with God) does not understand. Thus, the need for healing (Rev. 22:2)—to provide unity.

In Luke 19, Jesus also declared Zacchaeus as being *lost* (implying he was once with God, and then separated). The message of our being lost is woven throughout Scripture. Lost is not being able to find your way *back* to the place you originated from (God's fellowship in Eden).

Therefore, because God foreknew each of us *before* the foundation of this earth, and because we each sinned individually against God, as Adam and Eve did, in Eden (Paradise), and because this sin occurred *before* the expulsion from Eden (Paradise) into this world, then, Eden must be a place, created *before* this earth we now know (which is exactly what the Hebrew scholars tell us in the

Hebrew commentaries, the Mishnah, and the Talmud, concerning the Torah and the creation). In fact, the Bible itself tells us that *all* the host (or beings, of *both* heaven and earth) were *finished* by the end of Day 6 (Gen. 2:1). God's Word is clearly indicating two distinct creations.

God foreknew and predestined each of us. That means God knew our hearts in the beginning of creation and knows our hearts now. Before the foundation of this age, God placed each of us (the lost), onto a path to either be redeemed, reconciled, and repent, or to be permanently lost (Gen. 2:1; Matt. 25:34; Romans 8:29–30, 11:2; Acts 15:18; Romans 9:11–16; Eph. 1:4–5, 11; 1 Peter 1:1–2; Rev. 13:8, 17:8).

Redemption, in both the Latin and Greek, means to purchase *back* that which was *lost*, or separated from God. This means that each person was once known by God, and was then lost or separated, and Jesus paid the price of death to purchase us *back* to Him (Psalm 34:22, 103:4, 107:2; Isaiah 52:3; Luke 1:68, 24:21; Gal. 3:13; Titus 2:14; 1 Peter 1:18–20; Rev. 5:9, 14:3–4).[23]

Repent means to change direction, to turn away from the ways of this world, and to return *back* to the place we were.

Repent means to return *back* to the *top* (the best—Paradise), the *pent* house, return *back* to God (Matt. 4:17; Luke 3:8, 15:17; Acts 2:38; Rev. 2:5).

Reconcile means to restore us *back* to the relationship we once had with God (Romans 3:25–26, 5:10, 11:15; 1 Cor. 7:11; 2 Cor. 5:18–20; Eph. 2:16; Col. 1:20–21).

Why were we *lost* and separated from God?

Original Sin: We disobeyed God. Each of us, as an individual in Eden, sinned against God, and we are each individually responsible.

- God *foreknows* all events (Acts 15:18; Romans 8:28–30; Eph. 1:4–5, 11; 1 Peter 1:2, 20; Revelation 13:8, 17:8).

- God loves us all, and set forth His plan of salvation and justice (Genesis 2:1; Romans 8:28–30).

- God knew us all *before* the foundation of this world (Job 38:1–18; Jer. 1:5; Acts 2:23; Romans 8:28–30, 11:2, 7; Eph. 1:4–5, 11; 1 Peter 1:2).

We knew God *before* we were born (Romans 1:20–25, 3:12).

- We rebelled against God (Gen. 3; Isaiah 14:12–19; Ezek. 28:12–19, 31; Romans 3:12, 23; 1 John. 1:8–10, 2:2, 3:8; Rev. 12:1–4).

- God predestined us (John. 3:18; Romans 8:28–30, 11:2, 7; Eph. 1:4–5, 11; 1 Peter 1:2, 20

- God predestined His own sacrifice (Acts 2:23; 1 Peter 1:18–20; Rev. 13:8).

- God made this world we now live in for the redemption, the reconciliation. The creation is finished, and no new beings are being created today (Gen. 2:1; Job 38:1–18). We are born for the purpose of reconciliation and judgment.

Jesus said each separated being must be born into this world of flesh, repent, and be "born again" (receive our eternal spirit), in order to enter the kingdom of God (John 3:5–6).

And . . . here we are. . .

CHAPTER 4

CURSED AND BLESSED

GENESIS 3:16–19

For those who decide not to become a Christian in this world we live in, they must then, by all means, seek power, glory, self-fulfillment, and applause from the world around them. For the person without Christ, that is all there is—applause in this world, and then, eternal separation from God. Jesus will say He never knew them and condemn them to eternal separation (Matt. 7:21–23).

However, if one decides to become a Christian, then they don't need to seek the applause of this world, because they have blessings already, for all eternity, which makes the perks in this world pale in comparison (Eph. 1:3).

One issue facing our world today is whether women should be in the top leadership positions. Of course they should be, and are. Women are just as capable of leadership as any man. However, one issue facing the Christian community is whether women should be in the top leadership positions of the church. Of course not!

What? How can this be?

Jesus surrounded Himself with both men and women.

Women are equal to men under Christ (Gen. 1:27; Joel 2:28–29; Acts 8:12; Romans 3:21–24; Gal. 3:28). Women are just as intelligent and capable of leadership as men.

However, Jesus (God Himself, our Creator—Col. 1:15–18; Rev. 4:11) gave those that follow Him instructions that women (even though fully capable) must *not* be in the overall leadership position in the church (Gen. 3:16).

Why not?

God cursed both the man and the woman. Man is *cursed* to toil, to support, and to be the *head* of the family, to *lead* the family in God's ways, and is *cursed* to never be satisfied (Gen. 3:17–19).

Woman is *cursed* to bear children in great pain, and to *desire* to be the leader in the home, and also in spiritual matters. Woman, however, is *cursed to submit* (Gen. 3:16). Obviously, many men have perverted the last part of this passage of God's Word (submit), and have used it to justify evil deeds. But, this is just further evidence that those who so use it are not truly Christian. For if they were truly Christian, they would show compassion, love, and respect as commanded by God (Col. 3:19; 1 Peter 3:7).

The Hebrew term "to desire," in Genesis 3:16, is not a sexual reference, but a reference to *desire the leadership role* God assigned to the husband in marriage and in spiritual matters.

Many men, of course, try to circumvent God's curse by leaving the home, leaving the marriage, ignoring God, and seeking the world's ways.

Women also begin to circumvent God's curse, or the role God gave them, by endeavoring to become leaders of the home and church.

Men may succeed in the world's ways, and their wives may be forced to raise the children in God's ways alone, but these men are outside of God's will.

Women may succeed in the world's ways, and sometimes even divorce the husband for non-scriptural reasons, or endeavor to become the top leaders in the church, but these women are outside of God's will.

How can this be?

Man's sin is that he disobeyed God. Adam did not listen to God. Instead, he listened to Eve, and he did not take a stand for God. Had Adam reasoned with Eve, denied Satan, and submitted to God, then we would not be having this discussion. But Adam did what men generally do, he went along with the woman, and allowed himself to be swayed, to put God aside (Gen. 3:17–19).

Woman's sin is that she disobeyed God after being deceived by Satan. She listened to Satan over God. Had Eve conferred with Adam, and submitted to God, we would not be having this discussion.

All humans, both men and women, have sinned against God (Romans 3:10–12, 23, 5:12).

It is not that women are less intelligent, or less capable of leadership—quite the opposite. It is because women, in general, are so influential over men, that God cursed women to *desire* the top leadership role, but instead of acting on that desire, to submit or be out of God's will.

And, like it or not, men are cursed to lead and toil or be out of God's will.

Women are to submit in spiritual matters, because Jesus, the Creator, said so (Gen. 3:16; Col. 3:18–25; 1 Tim. 2:11–15, 3:1–12; Titus 2:1–15; 1 Peter 3:1–7).

The issue is not whether men are better—they're not. Rather, the problem is that men, in general, are weak where women are concerned. Women, in general, are so influential over a man's will that God cursed the woman's influence in the area of leadership in the home and church.

We must note that this by no means restricts women from achieving whatever level of authority they aspire to in the world, outside the home and church. God's curse, or restriction, is only in spiritual matters.

Today, however, women have abandoned God's commands because men have abandoned God's commands. Ironically, the men have led in this abandonment by shirking their responsibility, and women have abandoned their responsibility by stepping into the area that God forbid.

Statistics compiled in a survey by the Barna Group shows that women are 100 percent more likely than men to be involved in church discipleship. Women are increasing in the clergy, and many predict that the clergy will be predominantly a woman's profession by 2025. Today, in the mainline church, the seminaries have a female majority.

The Barna survey also shows that about two-thirds of church members nationwide are women. The reason many women in the church (founded by Jesus Christ) don't leave is because they submit to God (even His curse) and are patiently waiting for Jesus' return. Whereas, many men have left the church, abandoned their responsibility, and at the same time they have left God's will.

Some speculate that the reason so many women are in church, and men are not, is that women are spiritually stronger, and men today are spiritually weak. However, this is not the case. Rather, it is that, once again, *just as in Eden*, men who call themselves followers of God (Christians) have abandoned their role as laid down by God (Gen. 3:16). By not stepping up to his responsibility as leader, as laid out in God's plan for His followers in Eden, such a man is out of God's will.

The Christian woman who takes a leadership role is also out of God's will. She sees the opportunity to serve as an authority, sees doors seemingly opening, but in reality, in God's plan, she has been once again deceived into disobeying God's plan The reason many women argue for leadership in the church is because they will not submit to God and His command. They are deceived by pride and ambition in today's world (Gen. 3:16).

It is suggested by many today that the times have changed and women have advanced. Today we recognize women's equality, abilities, and contributions. We are all wiser today and more educated. *This is all true.* Is this not the exact temptation which Satan gave to Eve in Eden? Surely, today, it is okay. You won't surely die (you won't surely be out of God's grace). Do what seems rationally right. After all, God's command was for a different time, another age. Go ahead and do what feels right for you.

Just as when the Constitution of the United States was adopted, it established the ideal of all having equal opportunity. At that time, everyone knew that not everyone had equal opportunity. But, equality was an ideal to work toward. Eventually slavery was eliminated, women got the vote, and our country slowly evolved (and still is evolving) toward the ideal of equal opportunity for all. So, we humans rationally extend this argument to matters of God.

But, Jesus said not one jot or tittle of His Word would change (Matt. 5:18). Jesus said what seems right to man is folly, and that man's ways are not His ways (Prov. 16:25; Isaiah 55:8). God's Word is timeless. God's plan is that Christian men are to step up and take responsibility, and Christian women are to stand down.

We have come full circle. *An instant replay of Eden* is now in view. The difference being that Adam and Eve were ashamed (Gen. 3:7). But today *we* are proud of *our* achievements.

The irony is that leadership in spiritual matters of home and church is not about *our* authority. It is about *God's* authority.

To truly lead, one must die to self. The man must step up. The woman must encourage the man to fulfill his role as God commanded.

The church errs in its understanding of God's plan when it allows itself to be deceived by Satan into changing the roles between men and women in spiritual matters.

This is not a minor error. This is a critical mistake affecting the core of doctrine of God's Word and its effects have already opened the door to compounding error (such as abortion and euthanasia, homosexuality and adultery, divorce and re-marriage).

To submit as required by God, whether it be men to their role, women to their role, slaves to masters, or citizens to government, is to glorify God by our example of showing that our joy and blessings lie in a greater life (Eph. 1:3), not in this fallen world (Romans 8:18–23).

Let us now return to Genesis 3 . . . Eden, and witness how our sin affects our existence in Paradise.

GENESIS 3:7–24
The Curse of the Fall:

Genesis 3:7–8: Fig leaves are not good enough, as they represent man's work, and works will not save anyone (Eph. 2:8–9). God demands blood to cover our sins (Gen. 3:21—life is in the blood—Lev. 17:11; Deut. 12:23). Death will begin in the re-made earth (Romans 5:12), with our separation from God, and will be represented by the shedding of blood (Note: There are two reactions to this original sin in Eden: contempt, verses 4–5 and, shame, verse 7. Thus, the host are *predestined* by God according to their reaction to their *original sin* in Eden—contempt, or shame.)

Genesis 3:9–13: God knows all. God is asking us to reflect upon exactly where we are—lost. God is further testing the host of heaven.

Genesis 3:14: The serpent is cursed "above" (more than) other animals. Beginning here, animals are cursed, like man (Romans 8:18–23).

Genesis 3:15: Note that both the woman and Satan have *seed*. Bruise a snake's head and you kill it. This is the prophecy of the defeat of Satan.

Genesis 3:16–20: The Hebrew for Eve means "life-giver." "Mother of all living" is a *title* Hebrew scholars say indicates she will bear the generations leading to the Messiah—the source of the reconciliation and life with God. "Thorns" now come into existence—not before—no evolution is indicated.

Genesis 3:21: "Skins." The first blood sacrifice to cover our sin. Note that God does this—not man (sin has caused death).

Genesis 3:22: "Us." One uncreated, eternal God in three roles. See also Genesis 1:26. For a detailed study on the trinity, see my book *God's Plan / Satan's Plan*. Adam and Eve needed to be prevented from partaking of the Tree of Life, because if they did partake, they could not die, and would have to exist eternally separated from God. Only by dying (paying the penalty), could they *possibly* be reconciled back to God, and not be separated. They must also be "born again" (John 3:1–7)

Genesis 3:23–24: Mankind and womankind are preserved by God, after their fall, to be sent from Paradise to the reformed earth, which is *re*-created in Genesis 1:3–2:3 (the 7-day creation period). God's Word seems to indicate that Eve (womankind) could have had the ability to bear children in Paradise. This has implications for the end times and the millennium.[66]

Adam and Eve, two specific individuals, will begin the redemption/reconciliation plan of God for all of the fallen souls on the *re*-created earth (the 7-day creation). Creation will now change from the supernatural (eternal), to the natural (mortal).

- Note that the Genesis Eden account records all the host being created and in existence (mankind and womankind, Satan, and cherubim are all listed). Cherubim represent multitudes of the host of heaven (Ezek. 10). The 7-day account only reflects mankind and his presence in this world we now inhabit.

In Revelation 2:4–5, the church is warned to remember from where they have fallen. We have turned away from our first love. Gregory is quoted as writing, "We are fallen from the angels."[4]

Eden was not created for salvation. Eden was created for the host of creation to dwell with God in Paradise. And even though one-third of the host fell (Rev. 12:1–4), the rest of the host remained in Paradise. Eden is eternal and is guarded (Gen. 3:24). The cherubim in Genesis 3:24 were stationed to guard, protect, maintain, or keep the *way*, so that the saved would have a path (a way) to *return* to the Tree of Life (Rev. 22:2). They are not stationed there to keep us out. The age we now live in is the age of reconciliation/salvation. We are born for the purpose of being reconciled to God after the fall in Eden (John 3:1–7). In order to be reconciled back to God, we must first become flesh, and then spirit (v. 6). This is the age of grace and reconciliation for those who trust in Christ (Romans 5:10–11). This *re*-creation, unlike Eden, will be destroyed one day soon (2 Peter 3:10–11).

In Eden, we had free will—to either humble ourselves before God, or to want to become more like God. God gave us free will (freedom to disobey) so as to determine exactly who truly loves Him. God did create some creatures that follow *only* His voice, and who do *not* have free will, and these are called sheep.

With the end of this Eden creation account, we will now be moving to the next creation account, the 7-day account. First, however, we should consider the relationship of the created host of heaven (sometimes called angels), to the flesh and blood mortal beings of this earth. We understand that Adam and Eve (mankind and womankind) were originally created in Eden to live eternally. Adam and Eve existed in supernatural bodies while in Eden (eternal). Were these bodies like angels? We will resume with the transition verse (Gen. 2:4)—the transition to the 7-day account, after we discuss angels and humans.

CHAPTER 5

ANGELS AND HUMANS

"As for the mystery of the seven stars which you saw in My right hand, and the seven golden lampstands: the seven stars are the angels of the seven churches, and the seven lampstands are the seven churches" ***(Rev. 1:20)***.

O ne of the issues which confuses and clouds our understanding of God's plan (the creation, the fall, the reconciliation, and the judgment), is our understanding of the term *angels* and *man*. Are we in any way related to the angels of God's creation—the host of heaven?

An understanding of the creation and the beginning of our existence is essential in understanding everything else that follows the creation, including our need for salvation and a Savior. For centuries, scholars and theologians have struggled to understand exactly how the two creation narratives, which on the surface seem to be completely different, can both reflect God's creation. Some, over the centuries, have even suggested that one of these creation narratives is not from God, because they are so different in many ways. The truth of these two creation narratives lies in understanding how God speaks to us.

God speaks to us in riddles / parables, so that those who truly desire to know the truth will receive the truth. Jesus (fully God in the flesh), used riddles, or parables, in the New Testament (Matt. 13:9–17, 17:20). The God of the New Testament is the same God as the Old Testament (Isaiah 43:3, 11, 45:21–22). Some of these riddles / parables in the Old Testament include the story of Joseph (a typology of Jesus and salvation—Gen. 30–50), the rules for cleansing a leper (a typology of Jesus and salvation—Lev. 14:1–32), and the six cities of refuge (a typology of Jesus and salvation—Num. 35). In Genesis, God speaks to us in a riddle / parable concerning our origins. The 7-day account begins in Genesis 1:2, and the Eden account begins in Genesis 2:4 (The original Hebrew was a continuous series of words, but chapters and verses came into use by the fifteenth century, and the divisions can be somewhat arbitrary).

Most of us have formed our opinion of what an angel is based upon stories we have been told, or books we have read, and traditions passed down to us. What does the word "angel" in the Bible mean to you? The word angel in the Bible is *not* a reference to a being created different from mankind (adam—actually et-adam in the Hebrew—mankind). The Hebrew word "angel" is a reference to the various *functions* assigned to a person who is created to serve God. Pastors and priests are angels (Rev. 2, 3), created to serve God—their *function* makes them "angels" (in the service of God), not their *physical* status.

The Hebrew word "*malak*" translated as angel, means ambassador, teacher, messenger, or deputy—referring to their function, not their physical make-up. The Greek word "*aggelos*" translated as angel, means messenger, or pastor (Rev. 2, 3)—again referring to their function. The Greek word "*isaggelos*" means equal to, or similar to the angels (used in Luke 20:36), where in the resurrection we cannot die anymore because we will be like, or equal to the angels—eternal.

In Psalm 148:1–6, we are all listed together as angels, or the host of creation. All beings are angels (beings with a *function* . . . created to serve God). All the host (all armies and nations), are angels (beings with a *function* . . . created to serve God). All the sun, moon, and stars (symbolically, all the righteous), are beings with a function . . . created to serve God. All the waters above heaven (symbolically, all those who remained true to God at the fall, and did not sin (Gen. 1:6–7), are the host of creation (beings with a *function* (angels . . . created to serve God). In Hebrews 2:5–18, Jesus was made temporally lower than the angels (able to die), and we are compared as also being temporally lower than the angels (condemned to die), so that salvation and reconciliation can take place for all of us who sinned in the past (Romans 5:12), and who now trust in Jesus. The saved will be resurrected to their eternal state of angelic function.

Adam was an angel (defined biblically as a being created to serve God—a function). The only reference in the Bible to the creation of angles, or beings created to serve God, is in Genesis 2:4–3:24, where the host of heaven in Eden are first mentioned—mankind, Satan, and the cherubim, who were all created to serve God. Those in Eden are delineated by their function, not by their physical make-up (Satan's description as a snake is symbolic of evil, not a literal physical description). By the end of the 7-day creation narrative, note that all the host of heaven and earth are finished (Gen. 2:1).

God speaks to us in His word in riddles and parables (Matt. 13:9–17, 17:20). Whether we are called **angels** (Rev. 1:20; Psalm 148:2) **people, or armies** (Gen. 2:1; Ezek. 1:24; Rev. 19:14), **stars** (Rev. 12:1–2; Job 38:7), **host** (Gen. 2:1; Psalm

148:2), **trees** (Ezek. 31; Gen. 2:9), **stones** (Isaiah 14:19; Ezek. 28:14–16; Matt. 3:8–10; Luke 19:40; 1 Peter 2:4–5), **waters** (Rev. 17:15, 19:6; Psalm 148:4–6; Ezek. 1:24), or **sons of God** (Romans 8:14–19; Job 38:7), in Scripture—all are part of the host of creation. We were all created with the same type of supernatural *body* in Eden, and simply assigned different *jobs* to serve God, which is the biblical definition of the term "angel," not the definition we have invented today through traditions, and stories.

Whether we were all created with the same type of supernatural body, and simply assigned different jobs, is not totally clear in God's Word. Because of this, we should allow the Holy Spirit to lead our understanding of the host of heaven (who they are, and how we relate to them), rather than allow man's traditions to control our thinking. We must use the totality of Scripture to find the truth.

Were we once in heaven, and part of the host of heaven? Our understanding (or paradigm) concerning origins, begins early in life. Early in life, we are told angels come from heaven. They are here to help us. We are told they are invisible. We also learn that we humans are a special creation, and we are innocent little babies at birth. Later in life, we are told that angels are spirits (Heb. 1:14). We are told angels can "appear" human, but have no body. We are told that some angels fell from God, and these fallen angels are not eligible for salvation (Heb. 2:16—NASB; 2 Peter 2:4; Rev. 12:4). We also learn that we humans are all sinners (Romans 3:10–12, 23), and that we must be "born again" (receive our eternal spirit), in order to be reconciled back to God and Paradise (John 3:3–7).

Many struggle with the understanding that we once existed with God in Paradise, and now find ourselves separated (Gen. 2:1; Eph. 1:4–5, 11). At the same time, we know we once existed in our mother's womb, but no one I know can remember being there, either. Also, those of us who have a personal relationship with Jesus expect to exist in a supernatural existence with God in heaven one day (like being *restored* back to Eden/Paradise).

Questions arise: If our God is a loving and forgiving God, why are fallen angels supposedly not eligible for salvation, while fallen humans are? We know that salvation is planned from *before* the foundation of the world (Matt. 25:34; Eph. 1:4–5, 11; Heb. 4:3; Rev. 13:8, 17:8), and that the creation of *all* the host, of *both* heaven and earth, is finished and complete at the end of the seventh day (Gen. 2:1). So, who is God arranging to save if not the fallen host of heaven? To answer these questions requires us to open the Bible.

Does the Bible really say that babies are innocent? No (John 3:18; Psalm 51:5, 58:3—see *Original Sin* section). Does the Bible really say that the host of heaven is not allowed to be saved? No. The Bible actually points to a *reason* the host cannot be saved *while in heaven*. Jesus said in John 3:3–7 that two things are required for salvation. *First*, one must be born flesh, and *then* one must be "born again," or be born of spirit (receive our eternal spirit, the breath of eternal life—v. 6).

Jesus also revealed just a few verses later, in John 3:13, the plan of heaven (John 3:12)—that no human ascends into heaven unless he first descends from heaven—even, or like, Jesus did (becoming flesh). Some say Jesus (in John 3:13), is referring to His claim of authority concerning heavenly things by indicating that He comes from heaven. But, we know that this verse must refer to God's plan of reconciliation, because others have ascended into heaven (such as Enoch and Elijah). The context here is to both the physical and the spiritual, referring back to John 3:5–7, and the need to be "born again." The context is to eternal life (verse 15), for all of us who have been separated from God. Therefore, this verse refers to anyone being born human (mortal), and not just to Jesus.

We learn in Hebrews 2:14–17 that Jesus gives salvation to those in the mortal flesh, not those in the supernatural eternal state. Just as Adam and Eve, in their eternal state in Paradise, were expelled to this fallen temporary earth, and took on mortal flesh bodies (so as to die), so also, all the rest of the fallen host of heaven must take on mortal flesh bodies to have an opportunity to be saved. We must note that some (not all) of the fallen host of heaven did deliberately leave heaven on their own, while still in their supernatural state, and they are now bound in hell (2 Peter 2:4; Jude 6–7—see Gen. 6 section).

Why must Adam and Eve, and the other fallen host of heaven, first become mortal flesh in order to have an opportunity to be saved? Because it was while in the mortal flesh state that their sins were paid for and removed. Sin needs to be removed, and God requires death to remove them. Only a perfect being (God— perfect, sinless, uncreated, and eternal), could pay the price for our sin against a perfect, sinless, uncreated and eternal God, but God, being eternal, does not die. Therefore, God became mortal flesh (John 1:1–18, 6:33, 38; Phil. 2:5–8; Col. 2:8–9; Hebrews 2:9). In so doing, God (Jesus) actually became sin (2 Cor. 5:21), and died bodily, thus, eliminating that sin. An uncreated, eternal, sinless God could only become sin, and die to eliminate that sin, while in a mortal state. Because God is uncreated, eternal and sinless, and will not abide with sin, those who are fallen must either be separated for all eternity from God, or somehow be cleansed from all sin. Adam, Eve, and the fallen host must leave their eternal state, and become mortal to partake in God's plan for reconciliation. God loved us enough to lower Himself to mortal flesh for a short period, so as to suffer and save those who will trust in Him. All souls who reject God's love, and who do not trust in Christ, will be separated from God and sent to hell (eternal separation), for all eternity.

Ever since the Middle Ages, the traditional understanding is that angels and man are in no way related to each other in God's creation. This is because the understanding that we were all once part of the host of heaven *together* seemed too mythical after the fourth century, even though the *early* Christians viewed us as all part of the host of creation.

This same argument (about the *early* Christian understanding being too mythical), was also made in the Middle Ages, concerning how to interpret Genesis 6, and the angels who joined together with flesh women of the earth. Scripture indicates that some of the fallen host left heaven to take women for themselves on the earth. R. Kent Hughes, H. H. Rowley, Brandon Byrne, and Herbert Lockyer, all tell us that the normal usage for the term "sons of God" in Genesis 6 is to the host of heaven. (see the Gen. 6 section later in this book).[31, 56, 57, 60, 73]

The Scriptures tell us that angels *in heaven* do not marry, and also that in the resurrection, we will be like the angels (Matt. 22:30; Mark 12:25; Luke 20:35–36; 2 Peter 1:4). Jesus even remarks that at the judgment, those who deny Christ will be cast into the fire *prepared for the angels* (Matt. 25:41). What did the early Christians say? Tertullian: "We shall be changed into the angelic substance."[75] Gregory of Nyssa said the resurrection promises us nothing less than the restoration of the fallen to their ancient state, an angelic life.[4] Chrysostom said man led life like the angels, until the fall.[4] Gregory of Nazianzus tells us that man is a "new angel," meaning an angel now in a flesh body.[4]

Many wonder exactly why God uses such specific details like the 153 fish harvested on the right side of the boat in John 21:3–12. I'm not into all the number-counting schemes many get into, but John was inspired by God on a couple of occasions to use very specific numbers, both in the book of John and in the Revelation. Both the Hebrew and Greek languages used letters to refer to numbers, and numbers to refer to letters. Everyone recognizes that there is a letter-to-number representation in 666 used in Revelation 13. In the Hebrew, 153 translates to *beni Ha-Elohim* (sons of God—"angels"), just as used in Genesis 6, where the fallen angels came to women before the flood of Noah. In the Greek, "sons of God" is also related to the number 153. In the Greek, the term "sons of God" translates to 3 x 7 x 153, which means "The perfection of God's purpose is in the sons of God."

Here, in John, the *beni Ha-Elohim* are not the fallen angels who are condemned by God (Jude 6), but, are the *beni Ha-Elohim* who are reconciled and saved (Romans 5:10–12). God's precise use of 153 to describe the fish harvested into His kingdom on the right side of the boat is to inform us that we have all fallen (part of adam—mankind, and eve—womankind). And, just as Adam and Eve were banished to the earth to die as humans, we also will die—having been born as flesh humans. Yet, God will save all those who trust in Him (John 3:1–7)—the perfection of God's purpose—the reconciliation of the sons of God.

John Trench, in his *Notes on the Miracles of Our Lord,* noted that this "definite number, even as the number of the elect, is fixed and pre-ordained...being equal to the angels." Augustine referred to the 153 as symbolically representing the saved. Jerome referred to the 153 as the elect gathered into the kingdom of God.

The issue is that *some people* read God's Word to say that man was once part of the host of creation, but sinned, and has fallen out of God's favor. And, fallen beings are now being born into this flesh age, so that some can be reconciled to God (saved), while others of the fallen host will remain condemned (John 3:18, 5:25–29). Others *believe* that people are a completely different creation, separate from the host of creation, even though this is speculation, and not biblical.

Man is obviously part of the host of heaven, because the host, including man, were created as supernatural material beings *before* the end of the creation event, and this creation is finished...over...done.

- Genesis 2:1: Scripture says that *all* the host of *both* heaven and earth are *finished* by the end of the seventh day. What do the early Christians say? Basil the Great said that all beings were created before the foundation of the earth. Basil the Great also said that Eden is called our ancient fatherland, our homeland. Jerome said we were all planted (created), in the Garden of Eden as trees, together with Christ, the Tree of Life (4—pg. 55) [see the section on *Trees*]. Tertullian said that all souls today know of good from their pre-existence. God created all of us souls when He created Adam.[4]

- Genesis 2:7: Scripture says that in Eden, man was created as an eternal being (not to die). This creation event is seen, by some, as taking place on Day 6 of the 7-day *re*-creation event, and by others, as part of the original creation event of the heavens and earth (Eden), which was *before* the 7-day *re*-creation event. Either way, by the end of the seventh day, *all* the host of *both* heaven and earth, were created, and the creation is complete—finished. Some question whether Eve qualifies as part of the host of heaven, because references to female angels are missing in Scripture. However, in Zechariah 5:9, we read of female host of creation involved in fulfilling God's plan, which means Eve (a female being), also fits with Scripture, as a part of the host of heaven. Eve (bearer of life) was created to be an eternal being, like Adam (mankind). Male and female (as we think of them in this flesh age), are not significantly different in references to the host of heaven.

- Man assumes a flesh body, a mortal body, after the fall from Paradise (Eden), when man was banished from God's kingdom (Gen. 3:22–24). Whereas, the other host, who remain with God (the host of heaven, the sons of God, the stars which did not fall—Rev. 12:1–4), maintain their supernatural material bodies (their eternal quality). What did the early Christians say? Tertullian: "*We shall be changed into the angelic substance*".[75] Gregory of Nyssa said the resurrection promises us nothing less than the restoration of the fallen to their ancient state, an angelic life.[4] Chrysostom said man led life like the angels, until the fall.[4] In *Confessiones XII*,[17, 25] Augustine states that God made matter common to things visible and invisible. A spiritual substance has matter. Origen states in *I Peri Archon* (V1, p. xi, 170), that no created spiritual substance can exist that is not united to a body. Dionysius states in *De Divinis Nominibus* (Chapter 7, Lecture 4), Spiritual substance is united to heavenly bodies. The conclusion reached by Mary Patrick, PhD, and John Wellmuth, PhD, in their book *St. Thomas Aquinas on Spiritual Matters*,[58] was that spiritual substance is composed of matter and form. Augustine, in *Enchiridion XXIX*, states that all angels are from the same species (kind).

A common understanding is that God's salvation plan is not for beings in the supernatural angelic state. This *is* true. In order for the fallen host, or "angels," to be saved, they must first become mortal flesh (just like Adam and Eve, who were also created to be eternal). Jesus paid the price for salvation in the human, flesh state and shed His blood, the life force in the flesh (Lev. 17:11; Deut. 12:23). Jesus tells us that in order to obtain salvation, one must *first* be born human (born of water), and *then* born of spirit (born again—v. 6)—receive our eternal spirit of life, and have God, the Holy Spirit, indwell us (John 3:3–7).

Some *assume* that the reference to fallen angels being in hell (and therefore, not eligible for salvation), includes *all* the fallen angels. This *is not* true. Only those fallen angels, who left heaven on their own, are made reference to in 2 Peter 2:4. We read, in Jude 6–7, that those angels who sinned similar to Sodom and Gomorrah (unnatural), who came *directly* to earth (Gen. 6), are bound and held in hell. Likewise, in Hebrews 2:16 (NASB), when it states that God does not help angels, it is because salvation can only come through death (Heb. 2:14). Death is required for salvation (Heb. 9:15–28). The host of heaven are eternal. Only flesh, dies.

The fallen host of heaven, in order to be saved, must take on flesh as Jesus did, and face death. Not all fallen angels will take on flesh. Some left heaven on their own (Gen. 6), and many fallen angels will still be delayed in heaven until the very end (Rev. 12:9–17).[66, 68] Just as Adam and Eve lost their eternal state and were made mortal flesh beings (in order to be reconciled back to God), so, too, any of the host who fell, must also first become flesh, in order to be reconciled back to God. God became flesh through birth (Jesus). Likewise, the host of heaven must be born into this flesh age to be eligible for salvation. This is God's plan of love and forgiveness, to reconcile with the fallen host (Romans 5:10–11).

Jacob's ladder (Gen. 28:12) has been a mystery for scholars since it was recorded in the Bible. Many understand it to mean that God will send angels to protect people. While this interpretation is a possibility, the ladder is more likely a picture of the host of heaven coming to the earth and then returning. This image of the ladder is in the context of the descendants of Jacob (verse 14), meaning that the fallen host must come to the earth (be birthed into this flesh age), and trust in God, in order to be reconciled back to God (to return). In John 3:13, we read that no one ascends into heaven, unless he first descends to the earth (becomes flesh—John 3:5–6), just like Jesus did (the Son of Man, who is now in heaven again). Of course, just because one is born into this flesh age, does not mean they will be saved (see *Predestination* section).

The only reference in Genesis to the difference between man, the stars, the sons of God, the host, or the angels, is to our various functions, not our physical appearance. "Man" is to tend Paradise. Whereas, "angels" are described as having other duties such as being messengers. We were all host of heaven. The verbs used to describe the "human" role in the garden, though traditionally translated "to dress (till) it, and keep it" (Gen. 2:15), are the Hebrew words *abad* and *shamar*, which actually mean to "worship and obey" God.[55]

The word "angel" means "one who fulfills a function for God." The host of heaven (the stars, the sons of God), are given different tasks to perform, but there is no definite indication in God's Word that our being (our supernatural bodies), were different in the beginning. We are all part of the host of God's creation, and no others are being created today (Gen. 2:1). Therefore, a baby is not a new creation. In fact, according to Scripture, a baby is sinful, even in the womb (see *Original Sin* section).

Angel means "a being who fulfills a purpose for God" in the Hebrew. Angel does not mean a spirit being with no body (except for some wings), which is an image glamorized during the Middle Ages. In John's revelation from God (Rev. 1:20), the term "angel" is equated with God's messenger to each of the seven churches. The messengers to the churches are bishops or pastors (human).

However, some interpret the "angel" as being a supernatural material being from heaven (referring to their physical being, not their function), which John was to write to—not the bishop or pastor, himself. This would mean these seven church leaders were receiving their information from these beings (or "angels"), who supposedly got their information from John second-hand, and not directly from God.

It is true that messengers from God (angels) were often used to go between God and humans in the Old Testament, before Pentecost, before Jesus sent the Holy Spirit to indwell every Christian. But, John, here, is not telling supernatural angels what God says. John is writing to the messengers (bishops) of the churches (1 Cor. 3:16–17, 6:19; 2 Cor. 6:16). God did use angels to transport John to God's kingdom to witness the future events (Rev. 4), but the messages given to John were to be sent to the bishops, or pastors, of these seven churches—not sent to various supernatural beings. These are letters from John to the "angels" (bishops and pastors of these churches—human "beings"—messengers in the flesh). Some people may be angels (Heb. 13:2), indicating we, in fact, share much in common.

Also, in Revelation 1:20 and Job 38:7, angels, messengers, or people, are described as stars. This also occurs in other places in the book of Revelation, including Revelation 12:1–4, where it is interesting that the image of the woman has stars, and the dragon sweeps away one-third of the stars (one-third of the heavenly host fell). The woman has 12 stars (12 is the number in Hebrew for fullness, or completion—meaning this number represents the full number of the host of creation—i.e., the created beings betrothed to God, most of whom will one day be His bride—see Rev. 19). In Revelation 12:1–5, we read that from some of the stars (host) that are swept away, God selects His chosen (Israel), and from the tribe of Judah comes the Messiah (the Savior, Jesus), who was killed, then was resurrected, and is today, again, one with God the Father (John 10:30).

All this history is pictured in Revelation 12:1–5, using angels (stars), and humans, interchangeably. In Ezekiel 47:21–23, in the millennium to come, all the nations who trust in Christ will become one with the tribes of Israel again (the twelve stars *reunited* including all the sheep, stars, host, waters, trees, sons of God, angels, etc., who were lost.[66] Deuteronomy 32:7–8, v. 8 in the Septuagint reads "angels of God"—*ben el*—*not* "sons of Israel"—meaning that the fallen of heaven have become the nations of the world.

"Stars" are symbolically beings in God's heavenly kingdom, which possess a supernatural material body (as do all the host). Humans are beings on earth with a flesh body (to be resurrected one day, and receive their supernatural material body, when they are reconciled back to God, or judged and sent to hell (2 Peter 1:4). What did the early Christians say? Gregory of Nyssa said the resurrection promises us nothing less than the restoration of the fallen to their ancient state, an angelic life.[4] Saint Ambrose said the resurrection, as the very form of the word shows, is this: that what has fallen should rise again—the word is not erect, but resurrect—That is, to a supernatural state as in the previous age—Eden.[14]

In Genesis 2:1, God tells us that all the creation is complete at the end of the seventh day, including *all* the host of the creation of *both* heaven and of earth. The word "host," in the Hebrew, does not refer to some kind of angel spirit-being with no body. The word "host," in the Hebrew, means an "army of *people*," a "multitude of *beings*."

What did the early Christians say? Tertullian said that all souls today know about good from pre-existence. God created all of us souls when He created Adam.[15, 13] In Deuteronomy 4:19, Israel is warned not to worship the stars, or the host of heaven (those beings in God's kingdom in heaven). The warning is about worshiping someone else besides God, but the reference tells us that the host of heaven are also called stars. In Daniel 8:10–12, the host of heaven, the stars, are priests that are killed.

In Job 38:1–18 (this book is considered the oldest writing in the Bible), God asks Job a rhetorical question: *"Just where were you Job, when I* (God), *laid* (changed/formed) *the foundation of the earth, and when all the stars of heaven* (all the sons of God), *shouted for joy?"* Here the "stars of heaven" are described as "sons of God" (beings of God's creation, the host of creation), *before* even the foundations of the earth were laid or changed (Gen. 2:1).

R. Kent Hughes, H. H. Rowley, Brendan Byrne, and Herbert Lockyer all tell us that the normal usage for the term "sons of God," is to the host of heaven.[31, 56, 57, 60] When we are reconciled back to God and His kingdom, we will, once again, be called sons of God (John 1:12; Romans 8:14, 19; 1 John 3:1–2; 2 Peter 1:4). The Septuagint (Hebrew to Greek, three hundred years before Christ), translated "sons of God" (*"beni Ha-Elohim"*), as "angels."

God speaks to us in His word in riddles and parables (Matt. 13:9–17, 17:20). Whether we are called **angels** (Rev. 1:20: Psalm 148:2) **people, or armies** (Gen. 2:1; Ezek. 1:24; Rev. 19:14), **stars** (Rev. 12:1–2; Job 38:7), **host** (Gen. 2:1; Psalm 148:2), **trees** (Ezek. 31; Gen. 2:9), **stones** (Isaiah 14:19; Ezek. 28:14–16; Matt. 3:8–10; Luke 19:40; 1 Peter 2:4–5), **waters** (Rev. 17:15, 19:6; Psalm 148:4–6; Ezek. 1:24), or **sons of God** (Romans 8:14–19; Job 38:7), in Scripture—all are part of the host of creation. We were all created with the same type of supernatural *body* in Eden, and simply assigned different *jobs* to serve God, which is the biblical definition of the term "angel," not the definition we have invented today through traditions, and stories. All these terms are cross-referenced to man in God's creation in the beginning. In *Enchiridion XXIX,* Augustine wrote that all angels are from the same species (kind). In other words, all the host of heaven are common to one another.

Now, the host of heaven do not have a flesh body like we do, just as we will not have a flesh body (like the one we have now), when we are resurrected back into God's kingdom (1 Cor. 15:35–44). Scripture does, however, links us together.

Genesis 18:4–8: The angels washed their feet and ate food.

Genesis 19:3–10: The angels ate and used their hands to grab Lot.

Job 33:4-6: Job and Elihu recognize they were created out of clay (Eden), even though they exist now having been born flesh.

Luke 24:36–39: Jesus appears in a supernatural material body, able to be touched, and able to eat.

1 John 3:2: We will be like Jesus.

John 3:5-7: We are spirit, as well as flesh. God is Spirit, and Jesus is God, but also physical (flesh). We are both spirit and physical flesh in this age, just as Christ was, and we will be like Him in the resurrection . . . supernatural.

Luke 20:35–36: We will be like the angels (see Matt. 22:30).

Luke 24:36–43: Jesus said, "Touch me," and He ate with the apostles.

John 20:19–30: Jesus said, "Touch me."

Matthew 22:30: We will be like the angels in heaven—those of the resurrection. Note that in verse 28 the question was concerning "humans" when resurrected. Jesus answer referred to angels.

Matthew 27:52–54: Many were resurrected and walked around at the time of Jesus' resurrection.

Mark 12:25: We will be like the angels when resurrected (see Matt. 22:30).

1 Corinthians 15:49: We will be like the host of heaven.

Ephesians 2:19: We are fellow servants with the saints, and are of God's household.

Philippians 3:20–21: We will be like Jesus.

Hebrews 13:2: We may encounter angels without knowing it.

2 Peter 1:4: We will have a divine nature.

Revelation 19:10: The angel said that he was a fellow servant with us, and our brother.

Revelation 21:17: Both humans and angels use the same measurements (*not* NIV translation).

Revelation 22:8–9: We are like the sons of God (the heavenly host). The angel said he was a fellow servant with us and our brother.

Scholars understand that man was created with a supernatural material body, an eternal body, in Eden.

Genesis 2:7: Eden. The creation of man and woman is supernatural—eternal (Job 33:4–6; Isaiah 64:6–9).

Homilies of Chrysostom: Man led a life like the angels until the fall.[4]

Many scholars believe that the host of creation do *not* have a supernatural material body, but that they are *spirit only*. This is primarily because of confusing demons (which *are* spirits—evil spirits), with angels (see the section on demons in Gen. 7:21–24).

Hebrews 1:14: Angels are called "ministering spirits." However, this reference means having the spirit to minister, which humans also have. Humans have spirits, and they minister, but this doesn't mean they are a spirit being only. Humans are flesh and bone, and angels have a supernatural body. The Greek people influenced our understanding today. The Greeks believed that only the spirit lives on, and that the body is meaningless—evil. This leads to the view of bodiless angels, or host of heaven. This also led to the early practice of flogging the body, or punishing the body, as a way of striking evil (1 John 3:2; Rev. 21:17).

Hebrews 12:22–24: The general assembly of the host includes the myriad of angels, and all those already resurrected (the first fruits of humanity—Matt. 27:50–54), as well as God (Jesus). The resurrected are a part of the myriad of angels. The myriad of angels include the host, and those resurrected. Note that spirits of those awaiting the resurrection are listed separately from those already resurrected.

Acts 23:8–9: Spirits are *different* from angels. They are listed separately.

Scholars understand that man, when resurrected, will have a supernatural material body, similar, in some way, to the host of heaven.

1 Corinthians 15:42–44: We will have a supernatural material body, like the host of creation, who also have a body.

Matthew 22:30: We (those of the resurrection), will be like the angels in heaven.

2 Peter 1:4: We will have a divine nature.

Gregory of Nicaea said man needs to be restored to his ancient state with the angels before the fall.[4]

Tertullian said we will judge the angels that fell (1 Cor. 6:3). We will judge our brothers.[15]

At the resurrection to come, of the marriage of the Lamb (Christ), and His bride (Christians—all those who trust in Christ only), *both* the *host* of God's kingdom, and the *resurrected* (the redeemed of the earth), will be present *together*.

Revelation 19:1–10: All righteous (saved), will join into the marriage supper. *Both* the *host* of creation, and the *reconciled* of earth.

Matthew 22:1–14: In verse 10, *both* the evil and the good are invited, *both* the fallen (earthly), and the host of creation (heavenly)—see "Final States".[66]

John 10:1–18: Note that verse 16 refers to two groups of sheep: The host of heaven (those of the sheepfold of vv. 1–5), and *other* sheep (the lost which are found, and saved). Here, Jesus tells us that all will become one flock (see "Other Sheep" Message at Target Truth Ministries.com).

Most of us believe in some kind of life after death, but, how about this question: Have you ever thought about whether we existed *before* being born into this life, on this planet? In God's Word, in Ephesians 1:4–11; John 3:18; Romans 8:28–30; 2 Timothy 1:9; and 1 Peter 2:25, God tells us, in so many words, that He knew us *before* we came into this world. To help us understand this relationship with God (before being born), let's look at God's Word.

Jesus gave us three parables in Luke 15. The lost sheep, the lost coin, and the lost son. We should note first of all that in reading about these three situations (the shepherd who lost a sheep, a woman who lost a coin, and the father who lost one son), that the focus is not on the sheep, or the coin, or the lost son. The focus of the parables, Jesus tells us, is from the point of view of the one who was the owner of the sheep, and the owner of the coins, and the father of the lost son. In each parable, the owner is determined to be restored to the lost possession. The point of these three parables is that God is patient to wait for the lost to return to

Him. God is not quick to judge the earth, He is patient. But, one day, God has promised the time will be up (Luke 21:24–32; Romans 11:25–26). Thank God He has waited this long in history.

In thinking about this first parable (the lost sheep), turn in your Bibles to Isaiah 53:6–7, and note in the Old Testament, here (written 700 years before Jesus time), that Isaiah talks of the same thing. Also note, that this chapter of Isaiah also has a lot to say about the prophesy of the Messiah (Jesus). And, these prophesies were fulfilled by Jesus at His suffering and death—truly a supernatural prophecy, not of man.

The shepherd and the woman (in the first two parables), are seen as frantically searching for the lost. They each needed to find the lost item. The lost items represented value, and they needed to find them, or lose them. These are parables about God recovering what has been lost (us). But, does God have to extend Himself to us because He, Himself, needs us back, or does He do so out of His love for us? God does not need us to complete His existence. God created us for His pleasure, not because He needs us. But, God loves us, and is concerned with our being lost, and is patient in His plan to see us restored to a relationship with Him—to be reconciled.

In fact, God (Jesus) is willing to die for us. All of us, even though we are all sinners (Romans 3:10–12, 23), are valuable to God, and He desires that we all choose life (Deut. 30:19), and become "born again" (John 3:1–7 – establish a relationship with God – spend time with God). God wants to develop a relationship with us, spend time with us, and God wants us to develop a relationship with Him, and spend time with Him, so that no one remains lost and separated forever—permanently condemned to eternal separation—hell (John 3:18, John 5:28–29). We are each valuable to God, and He desires that we each be restored, or reconciled to Him. God says in Isaiah 55:7, that He will freely pardon us.

So, these parables are about souls being restored to God (if they change). We read in John 1:1–18, and Philippians 2:5–8, about God extending Himself to us by taking on the form of flesh, so as to die for us, a perfect sacrificial price, to pay for our sins, so that those who trust in Him, and spend time with Him, will enjoy Paradise with Him. God loves the sinner, just not the sin (our bad actions). He is waiting patiently for us to return that love, that desire to spend time with Him, and deny the world's ways.

In the third parable, about the lost son, note that sin is seen here, as the son takes several steps to walk away from God. These steps include rebellion against the father, desire for total independence (separation from the father), the waste of the inheritance, followed by a desperate need, and finally debasement and bondage. But, just as there were certain steps away from the father, there are also certain steps back to be restored and reconciled. In Luke 15:17, we see him awakening to his condition. While he was on his way down, he undoubtedly said to himself that his hard times were only temporary, and that his ship would soon come in. He imagined he still had friends. Even when he had to take a job with a detested pig farmer, he supposed he was only doing it on a short-term basis, until his bad fortune changed. The first step back was "coming to his senses." The second step back was making an honest confession of his sin. We read, in verses 18 and 19 of Luke 15, that the son humbled himself. He did not use excuses, or blame others. He openly admitted his sin. The third step was to return to the father (Luke 15:20–21). For us, this means being "born again," as Jesus says in John 3 (spending time with God, and developing a relationship).

There is another common theme of these three parables. They all refer to the "lost." If you think about it, in order to be lost, one must have belonged to someone, or had a relationship with someone, *before* being lost. Otherwise you can't be "lost."

In each of these parables that Jesus gives us, He tells a story of : the sheep existing with the shepherd, *before* being lost, the coins all being with the owner, *before* being lost, and the son existing with the father, *before* being lost. Throughout God's Word, He tells us that we need to be reconciled to Him to be saved, restored to His kingdom. Reconciled means to restore a relationship we once had, before being lost.

Paul wrote in Romans 1:21, about when people "knew God," indicating once again, a relationship with God prior to this age we now live in. In the context of Romans chapter one, Paul is pointing out how both Jew and Gentile (all nations), are fallen, and separated from God, and therefore, we now don't know God as we once did. Since we are all born sinners, having fallen, and are therefore separated from God at birth, this period of "knowing God" must have been in an age prior to this age we are birthed into now (Eden).

We know from Psalm 51:5, and other places, that we are sinners at conception, even in the womb. We know from John 3:18, that we are all born condemned already. We are all sinners, and that is why Jesus did not come to condemn us, because we are already condemned.

So, yes, God foreknew us all, and we are all lost. All sinners. All separated from God at birth. And we all need to be reconciled. We all need to repent (change) -- be "born again" into a relationship with God, and spend time with Him. *OR*, remain condemned to hell, separated, isolated, for all eternity . . . alone.

Matthew 13:24–30: Weeds. Jesus, here, is telling us a familiar story. A story told from the beginning in Genesis 3, in Eden, about the fall of man. Weeds are discovered in the field of God's creation. In verse 38, Jesus tells us the field is the cosmos ("world" in our English, but "cosmos" in the original Greek). Weeds and wheat are mixed together. Who did this? Satan. This happened "while *men* slept," as it says in verse 25. But, the translation of "men" (plural) is misleading. In verse 25, the Greek word translated in this case as "men," is actually a word that means "a certain man," and is a reference to God. In fact, this is the *same* word in the Greek as used in verse 24, "a certain man," *not* "men."

God scattered the good seed (the host of creation in Eden), and wheat developed (good--fruitful). Verse 25 is translated *correctly* as "while *He* was sleeping." This is how it is translated in the Greek Amplified English version, which is the correct translation of the original Greek word. This means that while God was resting, Satan deceived some of the host of creation (one-third, according to Rev. 12:1–4), and they are pictured here, by Jesus, as becoming weeds (unproductive). They have lost their eternal quality as good wheat, and have been "mutated," (damaged and corrupted), by false teaching. They have walked away from God, choosing the lesser good (self), rather than the greater good (God).

The fact that God rested, does not mean that He was not in control. Rather, God trusted the heavenly host to obey, and *allowed the host freewill* not to follow Satan. God *allowed us freewill*, rather than maintain total control over our will. God wants to spend eternity with whoever *truly* loves Him *freely*. This means that *we are responsible* for our decisions, because each of us made a freewill decision to either trust in God, or deny God, and accept Satan and the world's ways. God could have stopped Satan, but then God would have had to deny us freewill. God has given us our freewill, and we have made our choice (see the sections on *Predestination* and *Original Sin*).

So, here is the scenario of Matthew 13:24–30:

At the creation, *all* of God's creation in the beginning is good (wheat). All were originally created as good wheat, created by God, to live eternally in His presence. Some became deceived, and accepted the word of Satan over God's Word (Gen. 3; Rev. 12:1–4). Some wheat were essentially "mutated," or damaged by Satan, because they chose the lesser good (themselves), over the greater good (God), and these become weeds, unproductive, bearing no fruit. (Note that the heavenly host, and all the array of creation, are complete by the end of Day 7— Gen. 2:1). In other words, no new beings are being created today.

As part of God's plan of salvation, these fallen weeds (the damaged host of creation), are born into this flesh age, and some of them will repent, change back, become born again by the grace of God (John 3:3–7; Eph. 2:1–9), and are indwelt by the Holy Spirit, and will be fruitful, and finally harvested as good wheat, and spending eternity in God's kingdom. They *trust* in Jesus, and are reconciled *back* to God. However, many of these fallen weeds ("mutated" host), do not change. They do not trust in Jesus, and they remain mutated—they remain weeds (John 3:18), they will not produce fruit, and they will be weeded out in the judgment to come, to spend eternity in torment (being continually purged of sin) in hell (Matt. 13:30, 42; Rev. 14:14–20).

Most of us have formed our opinion of what an angel is based upon stories we have been told, or books we have read, and traditions passed down to us. What does the word "angel" in the Bible mean to you? The word angel in the Bible is *not* a reference to a being created different from mankind (adam—actually et-adam in the Hebrew—mankind). The Hebrew word *angel* is a reference to the various *functions* assigned to a person who is created to serve God. Pastors and priests are angels (Rev. 2, 3), created to serve God—their *function* makes them "angels" (in the service of God), not their *appearance*.

The Hebrew word "*malak*" translated as angel, means ambassador, teacher, messenger, or deputy—referring to their function, not their appearance. The Greek word "*aggelos*" translated as angel, means messenger, or pastor (Rev. 2, 3)—again referring to their function. The Greek word "*isaggelos*" means equal to, or similar to the angels (used in Luke 20:36), where in the resurrection we cannot die anymore because we will be like, or equal to the angels—eternal.

The scriptural support for man being part of the host of creation is clear, but seems too *mythical* to many. The scriptural support for angels being spirit only, from a different creation, and entirely separate from us, is very vague, but seems more *natural*. But, God's power and purpose is not limited by man's need for natural understanding and rationalism. God's plan is all about reconciling people *back* into a relationship with God—a relationship we once had in Eden (the original creation—Gen. 2 and 3). A relationship we have lost, due to our sin (the fall—Gen. 3:1–15; Isaiah 14:12–23; Ezek. 28:11–19, Ezek. 31; Rev. 12:1–9). We are born into this age (the 7-day *re*-creation—Gen. 1; Romans 8:19–23), already condemned to hell (John 3:18). Those who trust in Christ will be *restored* to a relationship in Paradise with God. Home sweet home.

CHAPTER 6

GENESIS 1:2 - THE TRANSITION FROM EDEN TO THE 7-DAY ACCOUNT

The earth now becomes formless . . . remade for the age of grace: After the fall, God transforms the supernatural earth (Eden), into a *formless* environment (*tohu wabohu*). Eden (Paradise) is now with God (heaven). This is the judgment of God, because of sin in Paradise. Isaiah tells us that God did *not* create the earth formless—it became that way (Isaiah 45:18), which means this verse belongs at the beginning of the 7-day re-creation event, where the earth is pictured in days one and two, as *formless*.

Some refer to this as a *gap* between Genesis 1:1 and 1:3 . . . a gap for evolution to occur. This is *not* a gap for evolution. There is no sun until day four of the 7-day creation narrative. *This is a judgment* on the fallen host from Eden (Paradise/heaven). This judgment occurs after the fall (Gen. 3). This "gap," is an unknown period of time. God re-made (*asah*), the earth into a "formless" (*tohu wabohu*) wilderness, and re-makes the heaven, as well, after the fall.

The word "And" in the King James, at the beginning of Verse 2, from the old Hebrew (*vav*, or *waw*), is used here to try and indicate a separation between verse 2 and verse 1, *not* to combine or link verse 1 and verse 2. Bible scholars have been divided on this from the beginning. The Hebrew can be translated either way, depending upon the context.[9, 4]

Some Hebrew scholars describe *vav* here in Genesis 1:2 as a disjunctive, meaning that they see this verse as a parenthetical statement—a comment on verse one, the creation. The comment is, of course, that the creation which had form (Eden), is now made formless (Isaiah 45:18).

The correct translation of *And* (*vav*, or *waw*), should be *But*. This is the way the Septuagint and Latin Vulgate translates it, because it is an adversative conjunction implying a delay, just as used elsewhere in Exodus 2 (8 years' delay), Deuteronomy 10 (38-year delay), 1 Chronicles 10 (7-year delay), and Ezekiel 6 (58-year delay). The introduction to the creation account is rendered in English by the *old Hebrew* understanding as: *"In the beginning God created the heaven* (singular), *and earth, v.* 2) **but** *earth* **became** *formless and void, and* **darkness** *was over the surface of the deep* **abyss** *and the Spirit of God was* **brooding** *over the face of the water, God said, 'Let there be light. 'And, there was light."* (emphasis mine).

The introduction to the creation account is rendered in English by the *late* Christian understanding as: *"In the beginning, God created the heaven*(s) *and the earth.* 2) **And** *the earth* **was** *without form and void, and darkness was upon the face of the deep. And the Spirit of God* **moved** *upon the face of the waters. And God said, Let there be light: and there was light."* (emphasis mine). This *late* Christian understanding actually does separate the first verse from the second verse, which is correct. In effect, they become two separate thoughts, two separate events. The conjoining word "And" here in verse 2, in the *late* Christian (King James), should be rendered "But." Even though they are two separate thoughts, to the *later* Christians they are viewed as linked to each other. *And* (*vav,* or *waw*) is translated as *but* in the Hebrew Septuagint (Hebrew to Greek, three hundred years before Christ). God did not create the heaven and earth in chaos and disorder, as described in Genesis 1:2. God created the earth fully formed (Isaiah 45:18).

We will come to understand that Genesis 1:1 is telling us God created (original creation) everything (this is written in the Hebrew in the perfect tense, indicating a completed task). Then, Genesis 1:2 tells us that the creation has been spoiled (the fall) resulting in the earth becoming formless. And then, beginning in Genesis 1:3, God tells us He *re*-created things during the 7-day creation event which follows the spoiled creation (this age of reconciliation—written in the Hebrew in the *"narrative tense"*—an ongoing event).

Here, in Genesis 1:2, the word "was," in Hebrew (*hayah*), should be translated "had become," or "became." The earth was *not* created "void," or "*tohu wabohu,*" it *became* that way (1 Sam. 14:17; Neh. 9:6; Isaiah 45:18; Jer. 4:23; Matt. 13:35; 2 Peter 3:7). Isaiah 45:18 is very clear. God created the world *not* to be formless—"*tohu wabohu.*" Yet, here in Genesis 1:2, God tells us that He had to make the world "formless" "*tohu wabohu.*" The Hebrew "*hayah*" ("was," "had become," "became"), is a transitive verb requiring action, and implies an active transition (as in Gen. 19:26: "Lot's wife became, *not* was, a pillar"). The Hebrew words for "formless and void," "*tohu wabohu,*" are in reference to God's judgment, and involve a delay in time between the fall (sin), and the judgment—just as in Exodus 2 (8-year delay), Deuteronomy 10 (38-year delay), 1 Chronicles 10 (7-year delay), and Ezekiel 6 (58-year delay). Unlike ancient creation myths, where deities brought earth into being through war and chaos, the Hebrew account is of God creating a Paradise from the very beginning (Gen. 1:1).

The fall followed the creation, and the judgment follows the fall. The Hebrew understanding is that the 7-day event which follows is *not* a creation out of nothing, as the *late* Christian understanding is—*ex nihilo* (18). The Hebrew position is that in the 7-day account, God used pre-existent matter (Isaiah 45:12—"made"—*asah*). Words like void, darkness, deep, and water, are all words related to evil, and to material existence, or re-creation, *not* a creation out of nothing.[18, 19, 20, 21, 40] The Hebrew meaning of "formless and empty" is not chaos, but rather *"waiting to be formed."* God's purpose is to begin to create order out of this existing disorder after the fall.

Remember, Genesis 1:1 is an introduction to the creation, and it does represent original creation (*ex nihilo*)—complete and perfect (using the perfect tense). Whereas, Genesis 1:2 transitions to a different account—the 7-day account, where God generally uses pre-existent matter. Eden is pictured as formed from the beginning, and the only thing missing is the rain and mankind (Gen. 2:5), whereas, the 7-day account is a picture of the earth being "formless"—"*tohu wabohu*" (Gen. 1:3–8), and finally receiving its form on Day 3 (Gen. 1:9–10). Obviously, Eden, *not* the 7-day, follows the introduction of Genesis 1:1.

"Darkness and deep"—"Darkness" is the Hebrew word "*choshek,*" which means misery, destruction, death, sorrow, and wickedness (Exod. 10:21). "Deep" is the Hebrew word "*thowm,* or *tehowm,*" which means to destroy—*deep abyss*—evil. These, together, refer to wisdom and truth being taken away from the fallen souls—a judgment. "Darkness" and "deep" are *not* a reference to oceans.

Note that in the Eden (Paradise) account, which actually comes *before* the judgment, God does *not* create any sea. This is just as in the new heaven and earth (Paradise—Rev. 21:1), where there is *no* sea. The waters below (Gen. 1:7), are beings (host), and are separated from God. Waters are souls, or peoples (Isaiah 17:12–13; Psalm 148:4–6; Rev. 17:1, 15, 19:6). The lost go to and fro in darkness (Exod. 20:4; 2 Peter 2:4; Jude 6, 13). So, the waters in the 7-day creation event to follow, are not referring "only" to material water, but *also* to "beings" (see the 7-day *re*-creation account which follows Gen. 1:2). God speaks to us in riddles and parables (Matt. 13:10–17).

The reference to God "moving" over the face of the waters, is actually a reference to God "brooding" over these "waters" or souls.[22] The Hebrew is "to brood." This brooding, of course, is the result of the fall in Eden.

God makes references to different ages/worlds (Eph. 1:21; Heb. 1:2, 11:3), such as the age of Eden—this current age of reconciliation and grace—the millennium to come—as well as the new heaven and earth to come.

In Job 38:1-18, God tells us that the sons of God witnessed the earth being "laid out." In the context of Job 38, the earth referred to here is *not* supernatural (not Eden). God refers to the "sea" (not part of Eden, nor part of the new heaven and earth—Rev. 21:1). The Hebrew word translated as "laid" means to "change," "impute," or "make," and is *not* a reference to a supernatural creation (*bara*).

The same word "laid," in verse 4 and 6, is translated as "made" in Job 38:9. During the 7-day creation event, the word "made" (*asah*) is used to describe creation out of already existing material—*not* original creation (*bara*). In verse fourteen, God states the earth was "turned," and this Hebrew word "*haphak*" means to "change," "overturn," "convert," "overthrow," or "turn aside." In Job 38:9, God talks about wrapping the earth in "darkness" (darkness, of course, means gloom). In Job 38:17, God speaks of "death" (shadow—darkness—this is not eternal life—this is *not* the supernatural original creation of Eden—this is *not* Paradise).

Obviously, the sons of God, here in Job 38, were witnessing the *re*-creation of the earth (after the fall of one-third of the sons of God—Rev. 12:1–4), as the context, here in Job 38, is to "change," "darkness," and "death," just like Genesis 1:2. Genesis 1:2, in the Hebrew, from the Septuagint (300 years before Jesus), reads: "*But, the earth became unformed and void, and darkness was upon the deep abyss. And, the Spirit of God brooded over the waters.*" (emphasis mine). God was *re*-making the earth for a natural flesh existence, to last for only a short period of time, in order to accomplish the reconciliation of many of those fallen from Eden.

God tells us, in Luke 3:38, that Adam was a son of God (Adam was in Eden—supernatural—eternal), but because of sin, Adam was cast out of Eden to this natural *re*-made flesh earth. For those of us who are "born again" (John 3:1-7), we will become sons of God—reconciled *back* to God after our separation, due to the fall (we will become like the angels—Matt. 22:30; Mark 12:25; Luke 20:35-36; John 1:12–13; Romans 5:10–11, Romans 8:14, 19; 1 Cor. 15:49; 2 Peter 1:4; 1 John 3:1–2).

There is no mention of length of time between Genesis 1:2 (the judgment when earth became formless and void), and Genesis 1:3 (the reforming of the earth in the 7-day *re*-creation period to come for redemption).

Satan sinned before man and woman. However, human death began with the 7-day creation. Therefore, the 7-day creation event (which follows the fall—alluded to here in Genesis 1:2), is the cursed creation (Romans 8:18–23).

In Eden, the animals were plant eaters, just as is described in the new heaven and earth to come. "Death" applies to those with blood. Scripture tells us that "life" is in the blood (Lev. 17:11; Deut. 12:23), therefore, "death" is in reference to animals and mankind—not plants. The plants had no thorns (Gen. 3:18), until the fall. God was light in the Eden account, just as it will be in the new heaven and earth to come (Rev. 21:23).

In the 7-day account, God will allow death, allow thorns, and eventually "make" (*re*-make), the sun, moon, and stars (which will not last forever). This 7-day creation is temporary, cursed, and groaning from the beginning (Romans 8:18–23—the curse is from the very beginning—verse 22 "creation until now"— and this is further supported by verse 29 "foreknew us" referring to the period *before* this 7-day creation).

Genesis 1 uses the name *Elohim* for God (power, Creator, majesty). Whereas, chapters 2 and 3 (Eden), use *Yahweh* for God (Lord God—Yhovah—Jehovah Elohim—self existent, moral, righteous judge). Also, note that the chapter and verse divisions were a result of the translations into English, as the Hebrew and Greek use no such divisions.

The best way to translate the texts of the creation event into English is to follow the old Hebrew and *early* Christian understanding. This would mean two creation accounts. And, now that science has caused us to review our paradigms, it turns out that, just like the flat earth paradigm, we now discover the Bible is again correct. Just as the Bible pointed out to us that the earth is round (even when so many thought it flat—Isaiah 40:22), so also we are given, in the Bible, a picture of God's plan, which leads us to the understanding that this flesh age is just an interlude, a temporary period of time for all those who have fallen to be saved—to be reconciled back to God, if they will trust in Jesus.

Eden is the original creation, and is a mirror image of the "new heaven and earth" which God has prepared for us after the resurrection to come—a restoration of all things (Acts 3:21).

Note that when this flesh age ends, the destruction will be like that after the fall (Gen. 1:2), where the earth will be made void in preparation to return to a period like Eden (the millennium—Rev. 19:18–21.[66, 68]

Before we begin to look at the seven days of *re*-creation, let me suggest the following as an appropriate reading of God's Word for these creation events (using, of course, God's exact words and meanings). If the scribes and priests of David's time had arranged the two creation narratives this way, God's Word would be clearer to us today.

Even so, for those who understand the two creation narratives, there is little problem in the *late period* English translation that we use today. God speaks to us in riddles and parables (Matt. 13:10–17), and all we need to do is study His Word carefully. Still, the current translation does invite confusion, especially because of man's tendency for naturalism today—including the general acceptance of *macro-evolution* which has become popular.[65]

CHAPTER 7

SUGGESTED CORRECT CHRONOLOGY

(Which is in agreement with the old Hebrew understanding)

The Introduction: The Original Creation Event Summarized:

Genesis 1:1: *In the beginning God created the heaven* (singular), *and the earth.* It was *not* created *tohu wabohu,* formless—which agrees with Isaiah 45:18.

The Original Creation Event Detailed—(Eden):

Genesis 2:4: *These are the generations of the heaven, and the earth when they were created in the day that the Lord God made the earth and the heaven.*

Genesis 2:5: *Now no shrub of the field was yet in the earth, and no plant of the field had yet sprouted, for the Lord God had not sent rain upon the earth, and there was no man to cultivate the ground.*

Genesis 2:6: *But, there went up a mist from the earth and watered the whole face of the ground.*

Genesis 2:7: *Then, the Lord God formed man from the dust of the ground, and breathed into his nostrils the breath of life; and man became a living soul.*

Genesis 2:8–3:24: The rest of the Eden account translation is inserted here.

Earth will now be re-formed for this age of reconciliation:

A temporary age (see also Job 38:1–18)

Genesis 1:2: *But, the earth became formless and void, and darkness was over the surface of the deep abyss, and the Spirit of God was brooding over the face of the waters.* (emphasis mine—Isaiah 45:18)

Genesis 1:3–2:3: Continue on using the existing translation of the 7 days.

Generations of this age now begin:

Genesis 4:1ff: Use the existing translation of the generations of Adam and Eve, and continue on. Refer to Appendix 2—Creation Comparison Chart.

Now, let us examine the 7-day *re*-creation events in detail:

CHAPTER 8

THE 7-DAY CREATION ACCOUNT

DAYS 1–7

Genesis 1:3–5
DAY 1
The renewing of the earth—Time for this earth age begins:

- Time, as we know it, now begins with the renewal of earth for the age of redemption (Psalm 104:30).

- "Light" is truth and wisdom. Only light is "good" (v. 4). Jewish rabbis interpret light to mean the Messiah, the Savior for this age (Isaiah 42:6; Isaiah 60).

- The first couple of days are mainly spiritual, not material. Wisdom comes before anything else (Proverbs 8:22). This was the view of the early church. On Day 1, God defines wisdom, truth, and deception (John 9:4–5).

- "Darkness"—lack of truth and wisdom.

- "Day"—those of the day—light, and truth.

- "Night"—those of the night—darkness, deception.

- "Divided"—souls from souls: truth divided from deception, righteous from unrighteous (Job 38:4–7; Jer. 1:5; John 9:4–5; 2 Cor. 4:6)

- Light is *not* a visible wavelength. The sun, moon, and stars are not visible until Day 4. God is light (Rev. 21:23, 22:5). Note that in vv. 3 and 4 God divided the light, whereas, in v. 18 it is matter (sun, moon, stars) that divides the light. Two different lights.

- Evening and morning—moving from imperfection to perfection, from disharmony to harmony, from darkness to light, truth, and wisdom (Daniel 8:26). The Hebrew root definitions are different from the modern conventional understanding. "Evening" in Hebrew is *erev*—decay, disorder, chaos, increased entropy. "Morning" in Hebrew is *boker*—order, decreased entropy.

- First day—a 24-hour period, as indicated by the phrase "*evening and morning*" and because God numbers them—indicating 24-hour periods. *Not* a 1,000-year day, as in 2 Peter 3:8. Even though the sun and moon were not "made" until Day 4 (*asah*—re-made), the Hebrew reference is to a 24-hour period. Whenever a day is modified by a number, it can only mean a 24-hour day. There are no exceptions (Exod. 20:8-11).[65, 74]

- Spiritual meaning—wisdom before material (Prov. 8:22).

- Day 1 could be the expansion event of energy into matter some call the "Big Bang." The universe does the bulk of its expansion in *less* than one second, according to science.[65]

- The earth is "formless" here until Day 3 (*not* the original creation—Isaiah 45:18).

Genesis 1:6–8
DAY 2
The firmament separates—waters above separate from waters below:

- God's message is still mainly spiritual. God is still the source of light. God has established wisdom and truth, and now separates the fallen souls, which Satan deceived (the one-third written of in Rev. 12:4), from those who remain true to God (2 Chron. 6:36; Psalm 51:5, 58:3; John. 8:23; Romans 1:21–23, 3:23; 1 John 1:8–10, 3:8; Rev. 12:3–4).

- "Waters" refers to souls (Isaiah 17:12–13; Rev. 14:2, 17:1, 17:15, 19:6; Psalm 148:4–6). This was the view of the early Christians.[4]

- There is no further mention of waters "above," here in Genesis. The waters "below" are fallen souls, and many will be born into this earth age (Exod. 20:4; Job 38:4–7; Jeremiah 1:5; Hosea 1:10; Matt. 25:41; Luke 19:10; John 1:11–13,3:5, 13, 17:5–6; Romans 3:25–26, 8:16, 19–21, 29–30, 11:2; Gal. 4:6; Heb. 2:14–17; 1 John 2:2,

4:10, 5:6–8—Note that verses 7 and 8 read different in the King James Version; Rev. 12:1–4). Some of the fallen souls will take wives directly, and are not "born" into this age (Gen. 6:2; 2 Peter 2:4; Jude 6, 13). Only the waters *above* are praised (Psalm 148:4–6). God planned our days (Psalm 139:16).

- The "firmament" includes the cosmos (v. 14–17), and the sky (v. 20). The "waters above" were *above* the firmament. This is *above* the sky with the clouds, and birds, and *above* the stars as well (Gen. 1:14–17, 1:28; 2 Cor. 12:2–6).

- The firmament is *re*-made (*asah*).

- Evening and morning—continuing to move from disharmony to harmony (Daniel 8:26).

- Note that on Day 2, as the waters were divided, there is no mention like other days that "it was good." God says only that "*it was so*," suggesting that, unfortunately, it had to be this way . . . because of the fall (Gen. 1:7). The Greek Amplified translation states "it was suitable." God "brooded" in Genesis 1:2 is translated as "hovering" "moving" and "moved" but in the Hebrew actually means "brooded." *God* "brooded" over this creation because God's paradise had been corrupted by sin requiring this temporary flesh age to save sinners. The *re*-creation is *cursed* from the beginning (Romans 8:18–23).

- The earth is still formless at this point until Day 3 (*not* the original creation—Isaiah 45:18).

Genesis 1:9–13
DAY 3
Waters are gathered and dry (land) appears. The dry is called earth, waters are called seas, grass is after his kind, herb after his kind, tree after his kind:

- God now moves from *supernatural* to *material* (worldly). The earth now takes form, as opposed to being "formless" (*tohu wabohu*—Isaiah 45:18; Gen. 1:2). This water and earth are *both* supernatural and *also* material. Dual meanings are common in Hebrew (God is moving from no sea in Eden (Rev. 21:1) to a material sea in this 7-day creation event). After the waters were divided and "it was so," here, in Day 3, God provides for us a transition which accomplishes two purposes at once. God transitions from *waters* as "beings" (Day 2), and transitions to *waters* as a natural liquid element, here in Day 3.

First, the water reference (here in Day 3), *looks back* to Day 2 and the waters, or "beings," being separated, which is also referenced in Psalm 148:4–6.

Second, this water reference also *looks forward* to the source of life for plants (later here in Day 3), where the water is seen as a liquid.

Both of these references agree with other Scripture. The first reference to waters as beings is supported by Psalm 148:4–6, and further supported here, when God gathers the water into seas, as this is what nations and peoples are called in Scripture (Isaiah 17:12–13; Rev. 14:2, 17:1, 15). And, the second reference to water (as liquid) is supported because, as we know, oceans are liquid, and separated from the land. God uses this third day to move from the supernatural to the natural. In the Eden account, *no* sea is mentioned—just like the new heaven and earth to come (Rev. 21:1).

- God, here on Day 3, speaks twice—once to conclude the creation of non-living events, and a second time to begin the creation of life events.

- Grass, herb, trees spring forth as from *seed—not* the Hebrew creation described in Eden. Note that these trees are specifically referred to as *fruit* trees, not described as the trees during the original creation in Genesis 2:9, which were pleasant for sight, to be desired (Matt. 7:17–20; Jude 12).

- Note these trees have *seed. No seed* is mentioned in Eden.

- Note that plants are created *before* people in this 7-day creation narrative. Not the original creation of Eden, where man is created *before* plants.

- Here, on Day 3, light for the plants is still from God (supernatural— just as Revelation 21:23, and 22:5 describes for the new heaven and earth— Paradise). Again, we are still in the transition from supernatural to natural, in this 7-day *re*-creation.

Genesis 1:14–19
DAY 4
Light to divide day from night—sun, moon, and stars:

- Now the creation becomes mainly material, not supernatural. This refers to actual visible light.

- Light is "changed" (*not* the Hebrew word for original creation of Genesis 1:1). Visible light for this age, as opposed to another form of light, or wavelength (Rev. 21:23, 22:5). Science knows most light from the sun and stars is *not* visible wavelengths.

- Note here, that matter (sun, moon, and stars) divided the light. Whereas, on Day 1, it was God that divided the light—a different light. If this were interpreted as part of the "Big Bang" event, then, as the universe expands, the frequency of energy stretches and the wavelengths eventually match that of the visible light spectrum— which is also being emitted from the matter that is forming the sun and stars.[65]

- The Hebrew word for "made" the sun, moon, and stars is *asah,* (*re*-made). Re-made from the original creation to suit the needs of this temporary age of redemption/reconciliation. Actually, the sun, moon, and stars were created in the beginning (Rev. 12:1–2). They now become visible during this 7-day *re*-creation event.

- The Hebrew writers did not use words for sun, or moon, or sea (singular), in verse 10 and 16, because these words in Hebrew are also the names of the Babylonian gods. Hebrew and Semitic, or Canaanite languages are all the same, and the Bible writers would not use the names of false gods in the sacred text.

Genesis 1:20–23
DAY 5
Creation of water life and flying fowl:

- The use of the word "creation" here is the Hebrew word for original creation (*bara*). Note that water life and *flying* fowl were not created in the period of the original creation of Genesis 1:1 (which is further described in Genesis 2:19—Eden). Original creation (or Paradise/ Eden), is like the new heaven and earth, which is also Paradise, and has *no* sea (Rev. 21:1). Therefore, these are a new creation for this flesh age.

The word *whales* used in the King James, is the Hebrew word for *monster,* or *dragon.* This is actually the first reference to dinosaurs in the Bible. The word *whales* is the Hebrew word *tanniym,* which means a hideous, huge, elongated monster or dragon. This Hebrew word is sometimes translated as *jackal,* due to its hideous appearance. The word *dinosaur* did not enter the vocabulary until the mid-1800s. The word usually used to describe dinosaur-type creatures in the Bible is the word *dragon,* or *beast.* Dinosaurs (dragons or beasts) were recorded by many cultures in the world, and even the Chinese calendar lists a dragon (along with the other eleven known animals). Marco Polo recorded that Chinese royalty kept dragons in preserves, and even brought them out for parades once a year.[65]

Genesis 1:24–25
DAY 6
God made beast, cattle, et cetera:

- These are reformed, "made" (*asah*), for this earth age. *Not* the Hebrew word for original creation (Gen. 1:24–25). The beast made here is the same beast made when God made mankind (Job 40:15—Hebrew *behemowth*—a large quadruped—a beast). Scientific evidence available today involving soft tissue, skin, and non-fossilized dinosaurs is pointing to thousands of years instead of millions of years for the age of the dinosaurs.[65]

- In Exodus 20:11, we are told that God "made" (*asah*), everything in the 6-day period. This is *not* the Hebrew word for original creation, but refers to the *re*-making of everything in six 24-hour days,[74] for this age of redemption and reconciliation.

Genesis 1:26–31
God *created* humans:

God here speaks twice on Day 6—once to complete all the creation of life other than that in His image, and a second time to create humans in His image—capable of making moral choices.

"Us"—"our"—One, uncreated God in three roles—see also Genesis 3:22. The Hebrew understanding of "us" is that this is a reference to angels conferring and carrying out God's plan.

Genesis 1:26 says God has decided to re-make (*asah*), Adam and Eve (mankind). God will re-make us from the immortal supernatural, into mortal beings, subject to dying, for the purpose of reconciliation.

Genesis 1:27 says God then "created" (*bara*), mankind as a flesh being (in place of the supernatural—Psalm 104:29–30; Isaiah 45:12). Every person now must be "born again" (receive their spirit—John 3:1–7), in order to enter the kingdom of God.

God's Word in these verses may not necessarily refer to "Adam" (a certain man), and "Eve" (a certain woman), who were displaced from Eden (note that in Mark 10:6, it states these were created from the beginning—no evolution). In Genesis 2 (the Eden account), mankind is created separately from womankind, but here in the 7-day account, both man and woman are created together. Here, the Hebrew word for man is *et-adam*—including the article *et*, indicating humanity, or the human race as a whole. Here, the Hebrew is not Eve, or "woman" (*ishshah*), but "female" (*neqebah*). For generations, many Hebrew scholars have stated these people (created on Day 6) were separate, different from Adam and Eve, the man and woman from Eden selected to begin the period of reconciliation of the fallen back to God.

Some scholars suggest that Moses was telling us only about the linage to Jesus, and was not interested in "other" people that God may have placed upon the earth. It is possible that God created many flesh humans along with Adam and Eve to begin His plan of salvation for those who are fallen from Eden and predestined to be saved.

The Hebrew word for original "creation" (*bara*), is used in these verses for men and women, not necessarily Adam and Eve who were "formed" (Gen. 2:7) back when heaven and earth were originally created—Eden. Note that Isaiah 45:12 states that when God remade (*asah*), the earth for this age that He newly created (*bara*), mortal humans of flesh and blood for this age of grace. Other creatures are remade (*asah*). God took personal care in the Eden creation (Gen. 1:1, 2:4). These of the six-day re-creation were "made" in God's image [v. 26, "made" (*asah*) implying the use of *already existing* characteristics (image), of God].

The Jewish view of God's image, is that we are able to make moral choices. Whereas, animals do not make moral choices. Those in God's image, make good loving moral choices, and those who make selfish choices, are not in God's image. Actually, humans born today, are *not* exactly in God's image (Romans 1:23, 8:29; 1 Cor. 2:14, 15:19; 2 Cor. 3:18, 4:4; Col. 1:15, 3:9–11). We are broken—a broken image. These, on Day 6, are "created" flesh [a new creation (*bara*), for this flesh age], by a distant command—remote, not personal like in Eden.

- Note that, here, men are to have dominion over the fish of the sea. In the Eden account (which is like the new heaven and earth in Rev. 21), there is *no* sea.

- Note that, here, the creation of people in the 7-day event, is *after* plants and animals are created. This is not the same creation period as man in Eden. God even emphasized this in Genesis 2:5 (Eden) when it states the original creation of man is *before* plants grew.

- The conventional interpretation is that these humans created here, in this 7-day event, are the Adam and Eve of Eden. But, God's Word does not necessarily indicate this. God says, in Genesis 2:4–3:24, that man and woman were "formed" with God's special "breath of life," in that original day of creation of heaven and earth (Eden—Gen. 1:1). With that "breath of life," God made man and woman supernatural eternal souls. Man was formed to tend Paradise/Eden (Gen. 2:15). Whereas, those created on Day 6 were created to replenish/fill (Gen. 9:1), and subdue the earth. Today, we humans must be "born again" (John 3:5–7). Two different creations, with two different purposes.

The assumption is made today that all humans begin with this single couple—Adam and Eve. However, the Bible does not clearly state this. The Bible states in Matthew 19:4 and Mark 10:6, that God created "*them*" male and female from the beginning. Male and female refers to Adam and Eve, but it may not exclusively refer to them only. In Genesis 5:2, God tells us that He called all of these *adam* (mankind), by using the plural term for both male and female as "them."

In the *Newsweek* magazine science section of December 1996, Dr. Carl Swisher, a geologist at the Berkeley Geochronology Center, reported findings which show that the existence of only one human species today is actually the exception in history. His research shows that the dating of various *assumed* ancestors of ours was incorrect, and actually various species of humans existed *together* for a time—all humans—all one kind.

In other words, science points to many couples in the beginning. These studies were further confirmed in 2011 by Randall Isaac, Executive Director of the American Scientific Affiliation (with over 1,600 members), as they state that the original population of *them* included a population of around 10,000. In Acts 17:26, we learn that God caused all His creation to come from one blood (one source). Neanderthals, and other species of our *kind*, went extinct.[65]

We are all descendants of Adam and Eve's flesh and blood, (the first humans of this age—whether a single couple, or multiple couples). We are all born of the same flesh as man and woman created here (*bara*—an original creation), in Genesis 1:26. The humans created here are souls, not "born of water." They are created new (*bara*), and therefore, are similar to man and woman from Eden. Commonly called Adam and Eve, they are predestined by God when created (Romans 8:29–30). However, *births* to these newly created flesh people (in other words, those that will be "born of water"—those born to these people as flesh beings), they must be "born again." That is, humans born into this world must develop a personal relationship with God, receive their spirit, be "born again," or remain separated from God, and condemned to hell (John 3:5–7).

The purpose of God creating these souls (here on Day 6), is more than to fellowship with Him, they are to "replenish and fill the earth" (have lots of babies).

And, each baby will need to be "born again," in order to be reconciled back to God. Obviously, this creation on Day 6 is different from the Eden account, because in Eden, no births (or need to multiply), is even mentioned. Whereas, in this 7-day event, there is the need to bear children, so that these children have an opportunity to be "born again"—reconciled back (John 3:1–7). Isaiah 45:12 says that the earth is "re-made," and man is "created new" (as flesh). Adam and Eve also have a very high purpose beyond having babies. They are to share the need to love God and worship Him with the future generations—share God's plan of reconciliation, forgiveness, and grace.

Hebrew scholars have been conflicted on this subject of exactly who these people, created on Day 6, were. Some say those created here, for this age, are more than just a couple, more than just one man and one woman, and that they form communities (like Nod, and the people Cain was afraid of in Gen. 4:14). They are to live along with the Adam and Eve of this age (the couple which God chose to use to begin His plan of reconciliation), in the newly re-made earth, and intermarry with each other.

Note that when God tells us of the generations of Adam, that He refers to these generations by the phrase, "in the day God created *man*," (this flesh age—Gen. 5:1–2, 1:26–31). Whereas, "Adam and Eve" (man and woman) were originally formed "in the day the Lord God created the earth and heaven" (Eden—Genesis 1:1, 2:4).

Either way, whether one believes these newly created humans are a single couple (the Adam and Eve of this flesh age), or whether one believes these are many couples (adam—mankind, and eve—bearers of life), God took (at a minimum), one pair of the fallen host from Eden, and gave them newly created *flesh bodies*, in place of their supernatural bodies, to begin this flesh age of redemption and reconciliation—from one couple to provide for the Savior.

The first use of "Adam" to refer to a particular individual occurs in Genesis 4 (which follows after Day 7), when God describes for us the generations which come from Adam and Eve for this new flesh world to provide for the Savior. Whether one is born from Adam and Eve, or from "other couples" (if one holds to that position), all need to be "born again" (John 3:1–7), in order to be reconciled back to God. All will die in these flesh bodies.

With this "Adam," sin enters *this world* (Romans 5:12). Because we know that Satan sinned *before* man, the fall had to take place in a different place (Eden). Adam is called the "son of God" (Luke 3:38), and all those generations after Adam are called the "sons of man" (Luke 3:38), until they are redeemed/reconciled. Then, they are once again referred to as "sons of God," just like the heavenly host (Romans 8:14).

- Note that in Genesis 1:30, God says "*it was so*." Again, indicating that, unfortunately, this is the way it has to be in order to reconcile with the fallen host. Genesis 1:31 says "very good," because this is the conclusion of the creation of this age for the redemption plan of God. This *re*-creation event (not man) is "very good," because this fulfills God's purpose. Man is a sinner, and distended to eternal separation without this plan of God to reconcile with us. According to the Midrash commentary on the Hebrew words "very good," this is a reference which implies "a comparison to God's created, and previously destroyed worlds."[29] The Greek Amplified version of the text reads "it was suitable (so), and He approved completely (good)."

God calls for all beings in this *re*-creation to eat only plants (see Gen. 9 section). God's intent is for no blood to be shed. But, because sin is in the world (Romans 5:12), and because the creation groans from the beginning (Gen. 1:2, Romans 8:18–23), death reigns (Gen. 4:8, 6:5–7). Romans 8:18-23 states "from the creation," and Romans 8:29 supports from the creation—foreknown (prior to this 7-day event).

Some suggest that here, at Day 6, is where the Eden account takes place where Adam is created, and then God creates plants in Eden. However, in Genesis 2:5 (the Eden account), God tells us that there are no plants *on earth* when man is created, whereas, on Day 3 of the 7-day account, *God planted the earth* before mankind was created. Obviously, Eden and the 7-day events are different.

Note that the Eden account records all the host of heaven being created and in existence (mankind, Satan, and cherubim represent multitudes, including man, Ezek. 10). The 7-day account only reflects mankind's presence in the world we now inhabit.

Genesis 2:1–3
DAY 7
Rest:

- "Rested" in Hebrew is *shabat*, which means "ceased."

- Verse 1 states *all* host, of *both* heaven and earth, are *finished*. The word "host" in Hebrew means , (as well as angels, array, stars, mass, army et cetera). Here, we are told that all things, and all beings, are finished (Psalm 33:6–9). No new souls are being created today . . . only flesh births to accomplish God's plan of reconciliation. Psalm 102:18 seems to indicate that there may be more created humans, but the actual wording is to future generations, and also to any new creations that God *might* (may) bring forth…not actually stating that God will bring any forth.

- God rested (ceased) from *both* the work He "*created*" and the work He "*re-made*" (Gen. 2:3). Again, a reference to two creations.

- Verse 3 states "created and made." Two different words, two different creations.

- The seventh day has no evening and morning. It is day only, meaning the creation was complete on Day 6, leaving only rest for Day 7—the creation completed. This earth flesh age will pass away one day, and all will live eternally—either in heaven, or separated from God—in hell (John 5:25–29).

The words used are *completed, finished,* and *rested*—all past tense. God is at rest today in reference to these days of creation, but is not at rest today in reference to being active in our lives—especially the incarnation and resurrection of Jesus. Hebrews 4:9–11, and Psalm 95:10–11 are a metaphor for work being complete leading to our inheritance—our eternal rest. The seventh day is not a physical time reference, but a metaphor for rest. The 24-hour rest cycle (Exod. 20:11), is given to us as a sample of what eternal rest will be like when our work is complete. The seventh day is a metaphor for eternal rest (no time limit), when our work is complete (Hebrews 4:1–11; Psalm 95:10–11).

As we are born into this world and begin to experience tragedies and suffering, we now ask the question, How could a loving God allow these evil things to happen? Let's explore this vital question.

CHAPTER 9

YOU ASKED FOR IT - SUFFERING AND TRAGEDY

God's plan is to reconcile with many of us who have fallen and separated ourselves from Him. God wants us back, and states in John 6:35–40, that He will not lose even one of the elect (those chosen to be saved).

Satan's plan is to either destroy the Savior from fulfilling His purpose, or if that fails, to use our fallen condition to try and destroy *at least one* of the elect, so as to set a precedent to overturn God's plan, thus establishing his authority over God and us. Satan continues to imitate God whenever possible, and distract our understanding of God's Word and promise of salvation. The battle began in Eden and will continue until the millennium ends.[66, 68].

Every day, someone asks the question: Why does a loving God allow tragedy and suffering to occur? Every day, a baby dies, someone contracts cancer, a major catastrophic event or some natural disaster takes place where people are killed. So, why didn't God intervene? Why exactly does God allow tragedy and suffering to occur?

And, there is another question which hardly anyone asks: Why does God allow Satan control over this world? The response? God allows Satan to control this world, so that we will be forced to make a freewill choice between God and Satan doesn't match with Scripture, because God does not tempt anyone (James 1:13—God does test the *saved*, but tempts no one), and God does the leading. No one seeks after God—we don't choose God, He chooses us (Psalm 14:1–3; John 15:16). So, there must be another reason God allows Satan to control this world (age).

The answers are actually obvious, if we look to Scripture. In the beginning, God created the heaven and the earth (Gen. 1:1). The original creation is supernatural, and the Hebrew word *bara* is used to denote original creation out of nothing. The heaven, the earth, and the host of heaven, are all created in the original creation. This creation, and the beings (host—sons of God), are all supernatural (eternal). Eden (Paradise) is a picture of this original creation, where everything is created originally and eternal (supernatural), just as the new heaven and earth to come in the future will also be eternal and supernatural. Eden is described in Genesis chapters 2 and 3, and Eden is very different from the 7-day creation of Genesis 1.

In Job 38:1–18, God tells us that the sons of God witnessed the earth being "laid out." In the context of Job 38, the earth referred to here is *not* supernatural—and therefore, *not* the original creation (Eden). God refers to the "sea" in this narrative of Job 38 (which is not part of Eden, nor part of the new heaven and earth—Rev. 21:1). The Hebrew word translated as *laid* means to "change," "impute," or "make," and is *not* a reference to a supernatural creation. The same word *laid* in verses 4 and 6 is translated as *made* in verse 9. During the 7-day creation event, the word *make* (*asah*) is mostly used to describe creation out of already existing material—*not* the original creation.

This is confirmed in Isaiah 45:12, where it states that when the earth was remade (*asah*), that God newly created (*bara*), mortal humans for this age of grace. In Job 38:14, God states the earth was "turned" (meaning "changed"), and this Hebrew word *haphak* means to change, overturn, convert, overthrow, or turn aside. In Job 38: 9, God talks about wrapping the earth in "darkness"— darkness, of course, means gloom (shadow—darkness—not eternal life…not the supernatural original creation). In Job 38:17, God speaks of "death"—obviously this is not Paradise (Eden).

Here, in Job 38, the sons of God were witnessing the *re*-creation of the earth *after* the fall of one-third of the sons of God, as referenced in Rev. 12:1–4. The context, here in Job 38, is to "change," "darkness," and "death"—just as in Genesis 1:2. Genesis 1:1 is the original creation. Genesis 1:2 is the earth being re-formed after the fall. Genesis 1:2, in the Hebrew, from the Septuagint, reads "*but, the earth **became** unformed and void, and darkness was upon the deep **abyss**. And, the Spirit of God **brooded** over the waters.*" (emphasis mine). God was re-making the earth for a natural flesh existence, and this 7-day creation to come is to last for only a short period of time (our time—this age), in order to accomplish the reconciliation of many of those fallen from Eden.

God tells us in Luke 3:38, that Adam was a son of God, but because of sin, Adam was cast out of Eden to this natural re-made flesh age earth. Those who are "born again" (John 3:1–7), we will become sons of God—reconciled to God after our separation due to the fall.

Most people view this world we live in today as God's good creation. Babies are seen as born innocent into this world. Every day, we hear of heroic acts where good people will sacrifice themselves to help someone in need. The image we have developed of this world is that life is a wonderful gift, and that we need to do all the good we can to persevere and develop it. Anything that harms our life (tragedies and suffering) represents evil, and God allowing evil just is not right—if He truly loves us.

However, God is doing the just and right thing by allowing tragedies and suffering, and allowing Satan to control this world. The reason why this is true is because *we asked for it*. We Christians need to grow up and state the truth. We asked for this! In the beginning, God created all the host of both heaven and earth (Genesis 1:1, 2:1; Job 38:1–7; Rev. 12:1–2). The woman represents all the host of creation (God's betrothed—the bride). Twelve is the Hebrew number for fullness, or completeness.

All the host of heaven (stars of the woman), are betrothed (engaged) to become God's bride (Rev. 19). While in Eden (Paradise—Gen. 2:4–3:24), God, our Creator, gave us all free will to do as we wanted. God wanted to fellowship with His creation. God set the Tree of Life in the creation to give us eternal life with Him, and God also set the Tree of Knowledge in the creation, and offered us a choice: either continue walking with God, and leave the Tree of Knowledge alone—or, choose the Tree of Knowledge over God, our Creator.

One-third of the host (with the urging of Satan), chose the Tree of Knowledge over the Creator. We read of the fall in various places, including the fall of Adam, Eve, and Satan in Genesis 3 where Adam, Eve, and Satan all sin, and are cast out of Eden to this age. In Revelation 12:1–4, we are told that one-third of the host of heaven (stars—those betrothed and engaged to God), are cast out of heaven to the earth. In Deuteronomy 32:7–8, we are told that the fallen angels become the nations of the world—verse 8 in the Septuagint reads "angels of God"—*ben el, not* "sons of Israel."

In Isaiah 14:12–19, Satan and his prisoners, the stones of the pit, are referenced. In Ezekiel 28:12–19, Satan is seen in Eden with the stones of fire. In Ezekiel 31, Satan is pictured as a great tree in Eden along with all the other trees of Eden, and some are cast into the pit. The symbolism in these passages in God's Word is clear: Whether the beings of creation are called stars, or host, or stones (stones of fire, or of the pit), or angels, or trees (bearing good or bad fruit, which Jesus described in Matthew 7:17–18), or "sons of God," one-third of the host (beings), of creation followed Satan. We chose Satan over our Creator.

God had made a commitment with us, that if we loved God more than anything (even the Tree of Knowledge—Matt. 22:37), that we would enjoy His kingdom forever (Tree of Life), and if we chose otherwise, that we would die (suffer a physical death and be separated from God—Gen. 2:16–17). Our choice was to follow Satan, and have knowledge, and be as God ourselves (pride). And, God has given us exactly what we asked for: Satan's way.

Scripture tells us that this world, this age, this earth we are born into, is Satan's domain (Job 1:7; Matt. 4:8–10; Luke 22:31–32; 2 Cor. 4:4; Eph. 2:2; 1 John 4:4). God gave us this earth age, because we chose to follow Satan. This age is only temporary. This age (world) is slowly dying and deteriorating, and death awaits everything (even the cosmos). We made a decision to die (be separated from God—Gen. 3). So, God, our Creator, has given us exactly what we asked for. We will all die to this flesh body, just as God's justice requires (Gen. 2:17). We are all condemned (John 3:18) to eternal separation from God from the moment of conception (Psalm 51:5, 58:3). We have all sinned (past tense, Romans 5:12). We are enjoying exactly what we wanted, Satan's way (this world), and not God's way (Paradise/Eden/heaven).

It is interesting that today Christians can accept the fact that we are sinners (Romans 3:10–12, 23), and that we are, somehow, personally responsible for our sin—but, we seem not to be able to say exactly why this is true. We hold onto views that babies are innocent, even though Scripture is clear that we are all guilty of sin from the very moment of conception. We are separated from God because of our sin when we enter into this world (John 3:18; Romans 1:21–32). And yet, we still hold onto views that we are basically good people. We know from Scripture that we don't seek God, that we don't love God, but rather God seeks us, and it is God who leads us back into a relationship with Him (Psalm 14:1–3; John 6:29, 15:16). Yet, we still think of ourselves as having a role in seeking God.

So, rather than blame God for tragedies and suffering, we need to point the finger of blame where it really belongs—right back at ourselves. We chose this existence (Satan's domain), and God is just in giving us exactly what we asked for—our freewill decision to choose knowledge of evil, rather than God.

Actually, the real story is how much God loves us (John 1:16–17, 12:47). We have already made our choice, and we chose to follow Satan. And yet, even though we rejected God, God is still extending His love to us. God does not have to do this. God is doing this because He loves His creation, and He is willing to sacrifice to save those who will trust in Him.

The Scriptures tell us that angels in *heaven* do not marry, and also that in the resurrection we will be like the angels (Luke 20:35–36; Matt. 22:30; Mark 12:25; 2 Peter 1:4). Jesus even remarks that at the judgment, those who deny

Christ, will be cast into the fire *"prepared for the angels"* (Matt. 25:41). What did the early Christians say? Gregory of Nyssa said the resurrection promises us nothing else than the restoration of the fallen to their ancient state, an angelic life. Chrysostom said man led life like the angels, until the fall. Gregory of Nazianzus tells us that man is a "new angel," meaning an angel now in a flesh body.

Jesus tells us in John 3:1–7, that to be saved and restored to a relationship with Him (to be reconciled), two things are required: First, *be born flesh*—a water birth—born of water. Those in angelic supernatural bodies (like Adam, Eve, and the host of heaven), cannot die. Therefore, the host of heaven who sinned (Adam and Eve are the example—Gen. 3:16–19; Revelation 12:1–4), cannot be saved while in their supernatural state, and they, therefore, must first become flesh—to die (just like Adam and Eve were cast out of Eden to die in flesh bodies—Gen. 2:17—see also Job 33:4–6). And second, *be born of Spirit.* Jesus tells us that we must receive our eternal spiritual nature from God—become spirit—John 3:6). Some will be born again (develop a relationship with God), but many will not. Those "born again" become sons of God—reconciled back to God.

Unfortunately, the Bible tells us that despite God extending His love, and mercy, and grace to us (Eph. 2:1–9), in the end, many (if not most will still not love God (Rev. 20:7–8). Many want to be in Paradise (want the benefits), but do not love God (Matt. 7:22–23, 25:1–13). God desires to save (reconcile), with those who love Him back. God wants to welcome us back into a relationship with Him (reconcile—Romans 5:10-11). But, if most do not love God, then God will allow them to remain separated, just as they have chosen (I call it "the great divorce"—which occurs just before those who truly love God, join Him at the great wedding celebration at the end of this flesh age (Rev. 19:7–9, 20:4–6).

In Genesis 3, in Eden, Adam and Eve showed that they were ashamed of sinning against God (they were humble). At the same time, Satan continued to show contempt. For those of us who will humble ourselves before our Creator, God is merciful, and will reconcile with us (Psalm 51:15–17; Isaiah 66:1-2; Eph. 1:4–5, 11; James 4:6). The rest (those who do not love God), God will divorce, separate from them forever.

Satan has done a good job of deceiving us into blaming God for suffering and tragedies, when, in fact, it is our own selfishness and pride which have separated us from God's presence, and delivered us into this deteriorating earthly flesh existence (Satan's domain). If it weren't for God's love for us, we would simply remain condemned to hell (separation from God) forever. But, God so loved us, that He took the step of sacrificing for those of us who will trust in Him. We don't deserve this opportunity for reconciliation, much less have any right to complain about it. Satan truly has done a good job of deceiving us into questioning God's ways, and questioning just who is really responsible for suffering and death.

Of course, God can, and does, intervene in history to accomplish His purposes. And, many times, our prayers are answered because they agree with God's purpose. But, basically, we are living the life we chose—Satan's way. Thank God that He is a loving God; otherwise, we would be truly doomed.

An understanding of Romans 5:12 is key to understanding that the Eden creation account and this age we live in today, represent two *different* earth ages—one supernatural (Eden), and this one which is temporary—flesh. Romans 5 is used by modern scholars to establish that we inherit Adam's sin (as well as our sin nature from Adam), in some way. In the fourth century, there was a shift in theology, concerning several areas of the Bible. This was due, in part, to the Latin Vulgate of the Roman Catholic Church mistranslating Romans 5:12 to read "*in whom all sinned*" referring to Adam, instead of the correct wording we are aware of today, which reads "*because all sinned*," referring to us.

Because of this mistranslation, Augustine formed a "Federal Head" doctrine position, where Adam is the head of the human race, and Adam is responsible for our being sinners, not us, and for over a thousand years, this mistranslated understanding has persisted. In the seventeenth century, Johannes Cocceius formalized the Federal Head position used today. Even though the translation error was corrected, no one has adequately reconciled this Federal Head position with the now-corrected translation of "*because all sinned*" (Adam being a Federal Head was *not* the view of early Christians before the fourth century).[61, 76]

Before the fourth century, the early Christians and Jewish people accepted the supernatural aspects of the Bible, but after the fourth century the church moved to a more natural explanation of scriptural passages. This movement to a so-called natural understanding included our view of the relationship of angels and humans, original sin and source of evil, the age of accountability and our supposed federal head, predestination, and our misunderstanding of the two creation narratives, as well as the true meaning of the *beni Ha-Elohim* (whether angels or humans) of Genesis 6.

The early Christians knew that we were each individually responsible for our own personal sin. In fact, the concept of the sin of Adam being imputed to future generations is foreign to Jewish thought (Deut. 24:16; Ezek. 18:20—the early Christians, including Paul, were Jewish). Erickson, in his book *Christian Doctrine* says, "There is a definite connection between Adam's sin and all persons of all times. In some way, his sin is not just the sin of an isolated individual, but is also our sin. Because we participate in that sin, we all, from the beginning of life receive a corrupted nature along with a consequent inherited tendency toward sin."

Donald Guthrie, in *New Testament Theology*, (1981, pp. 210–211), says, "Although Paul maintains that sin entered this world through Adam (Romans 5:12), Paul does not argue from the one (Adam), to the many (all people), as if he were heaping the responsibility of everyone's sin on Adam's head." In Paul's theology, we are each individually responsible for our sin in the past (Deut. 24:16; Ezek. 18:20; Romans 5:12). To quote Rabbi Joseph Telushkin, "The idea that every child is born damned for the sin of Adam is alien to Jewish thought."[63]

God's plan is to reconcile with as many of us who will trust in Jesus (Romans 5:10–11), while Satan's plan is to deceive us into believing that Adam is really responsible, and that we are somehow born good, have made a couple of mistakes, and only need to fix it somehow—not needing Jesus. Satan is continually imitating God, trying to substitute his ways, in place of God's ways. This began in the creation, in Eden, and will continue right up to the very end, when Jesus returns, and then, even further, at the very end of the millennium (Rev. 20:7–9).

Now that the *re*-creation is complete, the earth and heavens (plural), are rebuilt, and all souls to be created are complete and finished (Gen. 2:1), we begin to follow the generations from Adam and Eve as they occupy the re-created earth, to fill it with beings who are born into this world in hopes of being redeemed, or reconciled. Josephus stated that Adam and Eve's generations began to develop 2,262 years before the flood of Noah.[39]

One thing the Bible does tell us is that God *predestined* all this.

CHAPTER 10

PREDESTINATION AND THE MIND OF GOD

Because we were created in the image of God, and God is good, and God loves us, we assume babies are innocent. There is a complete disconnect between what we think about ourselves, being good, and what the Bible actually records. Babies are destined for hell. Babies are not innocent. All are sinners because all have sinned, and we are all condemned to hell at conception. Many people seeking truth reject a personal relationship with God, because God is presented today as arbitrary and unjust concerning those condemned to hell. God is seen as declaring us sinners at conception, seemingly without us being somehow personally responsible for sin.

In Christianity today, we don't begin with the understanding that we are all condemned to death because we are sinners, and responsible for our sin. Instead, we begin with the understanding that God loves us, and immediately find conflict with God's Word, which states He condemns us to death from conception. If we correctly present the truths of the creation, original sin, predestination, final states, and the millennium, people could clearly understand their personal responsibility for their sin, and their true need for the sacrifice of Jesus, and God's overall plan of reconciliation.

More than ever, in a pluralistic society where people are seeking truth, we are confronted by Christian understandings of how we arrive at doctrines or truths, which are loosely supported by Scripture, and are conclusions reached by good intentions, and the philosophies of man. For the person who can accept Jesus by simply learning that God loves us and died for us, there is no problem for that person on how we arrived at our understanding of truth and doctrines. But, even this Christian will have questions once they begin reading Scripture. Christianity needs to evaluate its own misunderstandings of how we arrive at our conclusions.

Ironically, I understand the conclusions of the doctrines or truths of original sin and predestination in the same general way as conventional traditional conservative Christianity. However, I understand from Scripture that the reason we arrive at the conclusions of these doctrines or truths is completely different from today's conventional Christian teaching, and it is imperative that our teachings represent Scripture, not philosophy.

Some common statements are:

"If God is such a loving God, why did He declare us sinners at birth, just because Adam and Eve (the first humans), sinned?"

"If I am a special creation, and God cares about me as an individual, how does He show His love by declaring me a sinner (even in the womb) before I'm even born?"

"Why should such a loving God command Joshua to kill everyone, even the babies, when he conquered cities?"

"Why did God kill everyone except eight, even the babies, in the flood of Noah's time?"

"Why does God save some, and predestine others to hell?"

Are these questions really representative of our God of love and justice? To answer these questions, we need to understand predestination, and it should not be so complicated that a child cannot understand it.

Martin Luther considered predestination to be the heart of Christian doctrine, the core of Christian theology. Predestination is central to Christian theology.

Many have no problem believing we will live in a transformed state one day in the future, in either Paradise, or hell. But, God's use of the term *predestination* in the Bible, suggests a prior existence of some kind (Eph. 1:4–5). Did we exist prior to being conceived in the flesh and being born into this earth age?

The book of Job is regarded by most as the oldest book of the Bible. Job was faced with both of these issues: life after death and existence before birth. Job believed in a resurrection of the dead to life one day (Job 14:14). And God, in a rhetorical question, facetiously told Job to *"instruct God, if Job understood, exactly where Job was when God laid the foundations of the earth. Tell God if you know"* (Job 38:3–4).

Of course, Job, without God's Word, like us had no understanding of this previous age, when all the host of heaven were created, prior to this earth age (Job 38:7). The context of Job 38:1–18, is to the *re*-creation of the earth. Words used are *laid*, which means *change*, as well as words such as *darkness*, *death*, and *turned* (overturn). These words do not describe the original creation of Paradise (Eden).

Many truths of God are not overtly stated in Scripture. The best known truth, the Trinity, is not overtly stated, but can be found if one searches Scripture. For example: Who raised Jesus from death? Galatians 1:1 reads, *"God the Father."* John 2:19 reads: *"God the Son"* (Jesus Himself). Romans 8:11 reads, *"God the Holy Spirit."* It becomes obvious as the Scriptures are explored, that all are one and the same.

In this same manner, Jesus spoke His truth to the disciples in parables, not overtly disclosing His message, but giving the believer just enough information to understand, if they searched the Scriptures (Matt. 13:10–11). And so, also, God's Word to us, on the subject of predestination is presented to us with just enough information, so that we can understand the truth of God's plan, if we search the Scriptures.

We understand from Scripture that we did exist prior to the foundation of the earth, but does this mean we existed in the mind of God in thought only, or in some state of being? In chapter 1 of his gospel account, the apostle John, tells us of how the mind of God, and the thoughts and expressions of God, the Word of God, the Logos, at the same time they are thoughts, can also be material. God actually became material in this age: *"The Word became flesh."* This was not a creation, but a transformation, as Jesus existed in the very beginning, being the uncreated God Himself (Col. 1:15–22, 2:9). God can create by speaking the words. God spoke and the universe was created (Psalm 148:1–5). God (Jesus), is the mind, the thoughts, and the Word. Whereas, we are a creation of that mind of God (Psalm 33:6).

The question posed to Job, is the question posed to us, when God speaks of predestination in Scripture, by saying that He knew us even *before* the foundation of the world (Eph. 1:4–5, 11).

God even prepared the kingdom for those who trust in Jesus before the foundation of the world (Matt. 25:34; 1 Cor. 2:7). Did we exist only as a thought, or did we exist in some actual state of being?

By understanding predestination in God's plan of salvation and judgment, we can come to a true understanding of our being sinners at conception, that God is not arbitrary, and that we have a real need for God's sacrifice and grace. In so understanding, we hope not to suffer eternal separation and isolation from God, and from the other host of heaven, forever (a separation commonly known as hell).

Scriptures indicate that we did exist prior to this age we are born into, and Scripture gives us a variety of examples to lead us to the understanding that we had a relationship with our Creator.

In Galatians 3:8, Paul writes about how the Old Testament *foresaw* the justification of some people by faith. This plan of God was established even *before* the foundation of the world (Eph. 1:4–5; John 3:18; 2 Tim. 1:9; 1 Peter 2:25). In Galatians 4:5, Paul writes of some being redeemed, and being recognized as sons of God. Redemption implies a previous relationship, because redemption means to purchase *back* that which was lost, or separated.[23]

Everywhere that the word *adoption* appears in Scripture, there are also the words *redeem, reconcile, repent,* or *predestine* within the context, all indicating a previous relationship (Eph. 1:4–5). In Galatians 4:5, Paul writes of adoption along with redemption. In the culture of Paul's writing, adoption had a different meaning compared to that which we now use in the modern west. Adoption, today, to us in the west, means taking into our family a person formerly unknown, and usually without any debt.

In the ancient world, a child would be taken into a home as a slave, in order to care for that child, and not necessarily adopted. True adoption meant being *revealed* as kinship, their old life forgotten, their debts no longer existing. That is, the debts are forgiven (paid), and that person now is eligible for the inheritance.[43, 44] As kinsmen, the sins of the sons of God are all paid, and they are now eligible for the inheritance.

In Galatians 4:8–9, Paul writes about our relationship with God, *"formerly when you did not know God"* The context is *this life*, referring to Gentiles worshiping false gods. The Greek *to know* implies a relationship with God. In fact, it actually indicates an *intimate* relationship, not just intellectual knowledge.[43] According to Alan Cole, Paul was very reluctant to write of humans "knowing God," because to know God (as used in the Greek), meant a close *personal* relationship.[43] Since we are born sinners, separated from God, this is impossible until we are "born again" (John 3:5). That is, *unless* we had a previous relationship before our conception. Paul emphasizes this understanding that we cannot know God, by restating his thought as, "be known by God," which clearly indicates that until we are "born again" in this life, we cannot know God.

However, after Galatians was written, Paul then wrote (in Romans 1:21), about when people *"knew God,"* indicating, once again, a relationship *prior* to this age we are born into.[70, 71] In the context of Romans 1, Paul points out how both Jew and Gentile are fallen and separated from God. Therefore, we *now* don't know God as we once did. Since we are all born sinners (having fallen), and are, therefore, separated from God, this period of knowing God must have been an age prior to this age in which we are birthed.

Theologians basically agree that the Greek words Paul used in Romans 5:12, means that each person, individually, in the past, turned from God. The *aorist* tense is used specifically by Paul to indicate a past action. Paul writes "we all sinned," pointing to a single *past* action by all, tied to the sin of Adam in the past. This same reference to *"all have sinned,"* (meaning a turning from God in the past), is referred to in many other passages as well.

Romans 5:12 also says that through one man (Adam), sin entered into the world (*kosmos*). Yet, we know sin existed earlier with Satan in Paradise (Eden), prior to anyone else sinning, and therefore, prior to this world. Adam did bring sin into *this world* (this age), but Adam, Eve, and Satan sinned originally in Eden. Indications from Scripture are that we, as individuals, did also (see also Romans 3:10–12: *"all turned aside, and together became useless"* and Romans 3:23: *"all have sinned,"* a *past* action). This is further supported in Romans 5:19, where we read that *"many"* were made sinners. This can only be true if the fall occurred in Eden (Rev. 12:4), where *many* fell (one-third), but *not all*. Otherwise, Romans 5:19 would have to read *"all,"* because all other passages tell us we are all sinners, even at conception—not one is righteous. In Deuteronomy 32:7–8, we are told that the fallen angels become the nations of the world—verse 8 in the Septuagint reads *"angels of God"*—*ben el*—not "sons of Israel."

Donald Guthrie, in *New Testament Theology*, 1981, pp, 210–211, states that "Although Paul maintains that sin entered this world through Adam (Romans 5:12), Paul does not argue from the one (Adam), to the many (all people), as if he were heaping the responsibility of everyone's sin on Adam's head."[79] In Paul's theology, we are each individually responsible for our sin in the past (Roman 5:12).

God provides us a clue to His plan of reconciling with us in the example of Hosea. Hosea (another Hebrew form of the name Jesus), is a type of Jesus, in that he pays a price to ransom his adulterous wife, *"again"* (Hosea 3). For Israel, Jesus will pay a price (on the cross—His blood), to offer salvation to them, and this will be the second time that God has offered reconciliation to Israel. The first time of reconciliation occurred at Mount Sinai (Exod. 19–20). And, this resulted in an adulterous act when Israel eventually rejected God. This results in the need for God to in essence, take an adulterous wife again, this time by paying a price on the cross. Jesus' sacrifice on the cross also paid the price to reconcile the Gentile peoples, who will trust in Him (Romans 5:10–11). When was it that we were together with Him, now requiring that Jesus pay a price to reconcile us back?... In Eden.

The words, *"we all sinned"* in Romans 5:12, are seen by some in the Jewish understanding (Paul's background), to mean that all mankind sinned because of their being descendants from Adam. The story in Joshua 7 is often used to explain the Jewish understanding of how one man's sin was linked to all Israel. One should note, however, that only contemporaries in Joshua 7 were included in

God's judgment, not future generations. Those who were direct family members, in existence at the time of the sin, were judged (*not future* generations of Israel). This Jewish understanding actually agrees with the understanding of all the host of heaven who were deceived, like Eve, being the ones judged as sinners, *not future* generations (Deut. 24:16; Ezek. 18:20).

In Romans 5:13–14, we are told that all are condemned to death because of sin, even though those generations from Adam to Moses were not guilty of sin in this life. So, obviously, they were guilty of some sin *in the past* (as they were not guilty of any sins, during their lifetime, which were listed in the law given to Moses later). Therefore, the sin they are guilty of is their sin in Eden.

The sin of Adam was trespassing (*abar*—Hosea 6:7), against the law, given by God directly to Adam—not to partake of a certain tree. The sin of Eve was allowing herself to be deceived, and missing the mark (Hebrew—*chata*, Greek—*hamartano*— Romans 3:23, 5:12), or falling short. Thus, all are sinners (*chata, hamartano*), even though many did not transgress the laws of Moses (Romans 5:13–14) as Adam did.

In Ephesians 4:18, Colossians 1:21, John 3:18, and 1 Peter 2:25, we read we are alienated from God, estranged away from God, again indicating a previous relationship. One cannot be estranged or alienated, without first having been together. Throughout God's Word, He points us to the relationship we all once had with Him. This relationship must have been in Paradise, because we are all sinners at birth, in this age, alienated and condemned at birth, and in the womb. We were created in the image of God, but we are born into this world as fallen beings, now in the broken image of God (Romans 1:23), separated from God (Eph. 2:1–3), and we need to be redeemed/reconciled in order to have a relationship again (Romans 8:29; 1 Cor. 15:49; 2 Cor. 3:18; Col. 3:9–11; 2 Timothy 1:9).

God uses words such as *repent, reconcile,* and *redeem,* over 200 times in Scripture, in reference to bringing us *back* from this separation, into a relationship with Him *again.*[23]

When referring to generations of peoples and nations which have turned from God, the use of the word *adulterous* in both the Old and New Testament, is used to point us to a relationship we all once had with God. Adulterous implies a relationship now broken, whereas, the Greek word for harlot, or prostitute (fornicate), would be used if the meaning does not imply a previous relationship. In Galatians 5:19 and Matt. 15:19, both terms are used, each referring to a different immoral act.

God's Word to us uses *adulterous,* to point to all generations which, at one time, had a relationship. Note that from the very beginning of God's command to Hosea, in chapter 1:2–3, Hosea was to take an adulterous wife (meaning a relationship had *already existed* there, and they were now separated). If Hosea had been commanded to take a harlot or prostitute as his wife, then the Hebrew word for fornication would have been used instead of *"adulterous wife."*

To be *betrothed*, for the Hebrew people was in essence to be married, except the formal ceremony had not taken place yet. Note in Hosea 3:15, the prophet was to *"again"* take an adulterous wife. The first time, was to symbolize God reconciling with Israel under the law and sacrificial system. The second time symbolizes Jesus paying a price to redeem us all.

Hosea is an example of the reconciliation to God, which Jesus makes possible by His sacrifice for us. Both Hosea and Jesus paid a price to redeem their adulterous wife. This is another way that God, throughout Scripture, tells us we have lost our relationship with Him, are now separated, and need to be reconciled.

God uses all these various terms to clearly indicate throughout Scripture that we are all sinners at conception because we all had already sinned against God, *prior* to conception.

Hebrew traditions are based upon God's teachings. The kinsman-redeemer (near relative), is one of God's teachings practiced by Israel, as in the book of Ruth. We are born lost (sinners) and in need of a redeemer. We were once children of God, but have all fallen, and are in need of a redeemer. Only a "near relative" to God can redeem us back to heaven. Jesus, a near relative because of our adoption as sons and daughters of God, restores those who trust in Him back to Paradise (Eden).

God has prepared a plan of reconciliation, a plan predestined before the foundation of the earth, to recover that which was lost (Eph. 1:4–5; John 3:18; 1 Cor. 2:7; 1 Peter 2:25). A plan to bring justice to a conclusion for those who continue to deny God, and continue to commit adultery, compared to reconciliation for those who repent and put their trust in Jesus.

Eden was not created for salvation. Eden was created for the host of creation to dwell eternally with God, in Paradise. Even though one-third of the host fell (Rev. 12:3–4), the rest of the host remain in Paradise. Eden is eternal (supernatural), and is guarded (Gen. 3:24). The age we now live in is the age of salvation. We are born for the purpose of being reconciled to God, after the fall in Eden. This is the age of grace for those who trust in Christ. This *re*-creation, unlike Eden, will be destroyed one day (2 Peter 3:10–11).

There are currently a couple of primary views of predestination, each based on Scripture.

One view points out that *Scripture states* that we all sinned and are responsible for our actions. God looks into the future and, through time, *foresees* and knows our hearts. From this *foreseeing*, God predestines us, before our birth, to be saved or not. In this view, God allows us free will, and He predestines us according to the free will of our heart, which He *foresees*. We are responsible, therefore, for our decisions, and as sinners, we are all subject to death. However, God saves some by His grace (Proverbs 1:29–31).

Another view points out that *Scripture states* that God is sovereign, and He saves who He wills. God chose us *before* the foundation of the world. We do *not* choose God. In this view, God predestines who He wills, and gives people either a heart to be receptive to His call, or gives them a hard heart. There is *no* actual freewill, *in this life*, on the person's part (concerning salvation), as we *never* choose God, unless He leads us (John 1:12–13; Eph. 1:4–5).

There is thought to be scriptural support for each of these views, but you won't find any resolution to these views in a theology class. You will find the answer in the Bible, in Genesis 3. Before God ever created this present earth age, He had predestined a plan for redemption/reconciliation, and God predestined each of us, based upon His *foreknowledge* of our fall, and of our individual responsibility in that fall. He *foreknew* us in the *past*—He didn't *foresee* us in the *future* (Romans 8:28–30; Eph. 1:3–5, 11; Rev. 13:8, 17:8).

God created us with free will. God created a free will host with which to fellowship. God wanted to fellowship with those who by their free will chose to be with Him. The early Christians understood that our free will was necessary for God to be just. Even though God is sovereign, He is also just. The early Christians understood that God created us to freely choose to worship Him or deny Him. Thus, the responsibility of sin belongs to each person individually.

God predestined us, based on His foreknowledge, to be saved or not (Romans 8:28–29; John 3:18; Romans 9:11–13). God is sovereign and creates us with a *receptive* heart, or a *hard* heart, based upon His foreknowledge. This foreknowledge comes from our relationship with God in Eden (*before* the foundation of *this* earth age), when some of the host, by their own freewill, chose the lesser good (self), over the greater good (God).

Evil was not a creation of God. So, where did evil come from? Part of God's creation was that God chose to give up His sovereignty over the host's decision making, and to allow the host of heaven their free will to choose God (the greater good), or choose self (the lesser good). God loves us, and God wants us to freely love Him.

God (the greater good), gave the host guidelines to live by, and most of the host of heaven chose to follow the greater good (God), and deny self. However, some of the host chose their desires (self, the lesser good), instead of following God's direction (Rev. 12:3–4). This choice (choosing the lesser good over the greater good), is the seed of sin. Focusing on self, rather than upon God, is the germ which led to the fall of the host of heaven.

From this seed of sin, grew pride and lust. Once our focus was off of God, we began to wander further and further away. Until today, we find the evils such as murder, rape, abortion, molestation, and genocide, all in the name of self. In fact, sin is so pervasive in the world today that much sin is ignored, and even seen as *normal*. Today, we tolerate, and in many cases celebrate, sins like greed, selfishness, boasting, drunkenness, adultery, homosexuality, abortion, euthanasia.

Today, there is *no* free will in this flesh age (concerning our salvation), because God predestines each person with a heart, based upon His foreknowledge of our freewill relationship with Him *in Eden*. God created the host (beings), with free will, so as to have a creation willing to worship, and obey Him, of their own free will—not robots. The one and only, uncreated, eternal God shows His willingness to give up sovereignty, as He became flesh (Jesus), and limited Himself. God freely, in His sovereign will, gave up His sovereignty when He gave the host free will (sovereignty), in Paradise, allowing us to choose between our Creator (the greater good), and the lesser good (ourselves). Adam, and the host, were created supernatural, created to live forever, created with sovereignty over their own lives—that is, until sin, and therefore death, had to take place.

God foreknew that some of the host He created, would turn away from Him and disobey His commands, because He gave us free will.

In the very beginning, man and woman were created in God's image, but ever since the creation was finished, on Day 6 (Gen. 2:1), no one is *born* in God's image. Because God loves us so much, He provides this life opportunity so that some may be reconciled back to Him.

Today, therefore, we are born into this age of grace, having no relationship with God when we are born (Eph. 2:1; James 2:26), and having no free will concerning our salvation. Whereas, in Eden, we lived with God in an eternal state, having free will concerning our relationship with God or Satan. *Many* were deceived in Eden, and chose to disobey God. In this age of grace (unmerited favor), there are no works one can perform to achieve salvation (Eph. 2:8–9). God is sovereign, and He determines mercy.

God is just. God foreknew Pharaoh had a hard heart (from Eden), and thus, gave him a hard heart at birth, yet Pharaoh is responsible for his actions (from Eden), just as we all are.

So, why do we have to go through this birth, and life, and death? After all, God already knows who is to be saved and who is not. So, what's the point? Why did God birth us with hearts that match our sin? Why not just declare us saved, or send us to hell? If God already knows the result, why do we go through this?

Just as with prayer, when God already knows our prayers even before we pray (Matt. 6:8), we pray to put ourselves in agreement with God, likewise, we need to go through this age to put ourselves in agreement with God. We become partners in the decision, as we are led by the Holy Spirit, to transform our minds. We are being prepared for reconciliation. For better or worse, through this life experience, we are brought into understanding and agreement with God's judgment. Also, this is God's way of loving even those who turned from Him. The price of death is due to cover our sin. God loves us enough to die for us. Salvation is not available to anyone, unless the price to cover our sins is paid—thus, the need for this age, to pay the penalty of death.

Unfortunately, not everyone is called to salvation in this age we now live, which is the fault of man. God, from the very beginning, gave Adam the truth to pass on to all generations. So, another period is necessary to provide for those who we fail to reach. God doesn't intend to interfere, in this age, and allows man to do his best. Even though we fail to spread the gospel to all humans, God's plan has arranged for those who were missed, to hear the call to salvation. It's called the millennium, where those missed during the long harvest will be *gleaned* (Lev. 23:22).

God does inwardly call certain elect (chosen), in this flesh age by the Holy Spirit and direct revelation—for example: Abraham, Moses, Paul—in order to accomplish His purpose (Romans 8:28–29). Other than those specifically called to accomplish God's plan, all others are called outwardly by the gospel. Christians are commanded to spread the gospel to all peoples in order that they be saved.

Because many are deceived, or never hear the call (which is man's fault), God has provided the millennium (a period of gleaning—Rev. 20:4–15), where all will exist in a supernatural state, where Christ will reign supreme, where all will be called to salvation, and where, at the end of the millennium, Jesus will issue a final judgment.

This is God's plan, which even a *child* can understand:

God created heaven and earth—Eden / Paradise, and all host.

Those who obeyed, those who stayed true to God, they remain in Paradise (Rev. 12:1-4—two-thirds; Job 38:7). These choose the greater good (God), over the lesser good (self).

Those who disobeyed, chose the lesser good (self), but also showed *shame* in Paradise (such as Adam and Eve in Eden—Gen. 3:7–8), are condemned to die, and banished to the cursed earth to be called to salvation.

Those who disobeyed, chose the lesser good (self), and showed *hostility* and *contempt* in Paradise (Satan—Isaiah 14:12–15), are banished to the cursed earth and are judged *non-elect*, and *predestined to eternal separation* from God (Romans

9:11v13, 22; John 3:18; Rev. 13:8, 17:8, 20:14–15; John 6:70; Isaiah 66:24; Prov. 16:4; 1 Peter 2:8; Jude 4).

Those that abandoned their first estate (Eden/Paradise—Gen. 6:1-6), are bound awaiting the judgment (1 Peter. 2:4; Jude 6).

Some angels remain until the very end (Rev. 12:9).

The creation of all beings is finished at the end of the sixth day (Genesis 2:1). God knows the exact number to be saved, because He knows how many fell (Luke 21:24; Acts 17:31; Romans 11:25; Rev. 12:1-4—one-third). God even prepared the kingdom for those who trust in Jesus *before* the foundation of the world—this age (Matt. 25:34; 1 Cor. 2:7).

Those who are never called to salvation during this flesh age—those who never hear the gospel message of salvation (which is man's fault), such as the aborted, deceived, lost, etc., will be called to the gospel of salvation during the millennium—the gleaning of the long harvest (Lev. 23:22)…but that is another story . . . [66,68]

See Appendix 1 for Predestination Scripture List

All are predestined, that is, all will be called (Matt. 13:1–9), in one form or another, as God loves all and wants none to perish. God elected some, predestined some, set some on a specific path into this earth age in His plan of redemption. God specifically chose some to redemption, elected to reclaim certain ones back to Him, in this flesh age. All will be called. Not all will be saved. All will hear the message of eternal life through Jesus Christ (Isaiah 45:22, 49:6, Matt. 13, 24:14, Mark 13:10, Luke 16:19–31, Acts 2:31–33, Eph. 4:7-10, 1 Peter 3:18–22). Some will reject the call (Rev. 13:8, 17:8, 22:19).

Certain elect will be called during their lifetime in this current flesh age. The remainder either: A) received the call at the resurrection of Christ; B) will receive their call in the millennium to come, or C) received the call to salvation during their lifetime and made a decision to reject Jesus (see Final States Study).[66] Those who do not reject the call, will, by God's grace, be given the ability to have faith and trust only in Jesus. Their names will not be blotted out of the Book of Life, and they will proceed on a path of change (repent and sanctification), from the world's ways to the ways of God. Those who persist and endure, even though they falter, will by God's grace (Eph. 2:8–9) be saved (salvation), from being eternally separated from God. Merely abiding in, or partaking of the Holy Spirit, is not the same as receiving and accepting Jesus. One must receive Jesus, and not reject Him. Salvation and faith are gifts, and cannot be earned (Isaiah 12:2).

Being a sinner after receiving salvation will not separate one from God. All are sinners in this mortal flesh body, and Jesus paid the price for all sin in full, for those who will trust in Him. Sinning is not rejecting God. Sinning is falling short, missing the mark. Only those who reject the call (rejecting God), will perish.

The saved are made just before God (justified), by the grace of God, and the shedding of the blood of Jesus, and His death in our place (atonement).

● Jesus has redeemed/reconciled us, paid the price of sin, which is death, and He paid it in full (redemption, John 19:30— reconciliation, Romans 5:10-11).

To be saved is to be born anew spiritually ("born again"— John 3:1-7), and to receive one's eternal spirit from God, even though we, for a time, will still remain in a mortal flesh body, and still be subject to sinning, and will still need to repent.

Those who have been justified by Jesus, God the Son, are made right (righteous), with God the Father, and those God justifies are then set apart from the world (sanctified). Sanctification is a day-by-day process throughout life. At the return of Jesus to this world, the saved will receive their eternal resurrection body (glorified).

In Matthew 13, Jesus tells us of the Word of God, (seed), being given to four types of soils (people). All are given the seed (called), however, only one soil (person), is receptive to the Word and continues to trust in the Word. One soil appears deceived, and has the seed stolen by Satan (birds). Two other soils seem to hear the call, and partake of the seed, but then in time, they allow the Word to die in their hearts. They abide and partake of the Word, but do not receive and trust in Jesus.

God does the calling, and the justifying, and the sanctifying. All we do is decide to reject Jesus, or be receptive, trust and receive Him.

Salvation is like sap. One must continue to stay in touch with the source of the sap (Jesus, the true vine), or perish if we depart from it (John 15:5–6, Romans 11:16–22).

Let's review all the various beings which we find in God's plan, as it unfolds from the creation, to the final judgment and destruction.

God's perfect will is to create a perfect, good, freewill host to fellowship with for all eternity (Gen. 1:1, 2, 3; Job. 38:1–18; Jer. 1:5; Ezek. 28:13–16; Acts 2:23; Romans 1. 8, 11; Gal. 4:6; Eph. 1:4–5, 11; 1 John 1, Rev. 12:1–4—see the *Eden* section, and the *Angels* section).

God has foreknowledge of all time, and knows that some (one-third of the host) will choose evil. God predestines a plan of judgment and redemption through Jesus to provide for the fulfillment of His will (Eph. 1:4–5, 11; Romans 8, 11; Rev. 12:1–4).

God has foreknowledge of good, evil, and the freewill decisions of the host, both for and against His perfect will (Eph. 1, 1 Peter 1). Note: in Genesis 3 in Paradise (Eden), the host show their heart to God: A) shame—verse 7, B) hostility—verse 14.

God says we, the fallen host, have all sinned, and He foreknew this. In each case, in the original Greek, in Romans 3:12, 5:12; 1 Peter 1; Eph. 1; and 2 Thess. 2:13, the Greek indicates a relationship between God and each of us *before* the creation of this earth age we have been born into.[10, 42]

God begins His plan of judgment and redemption, through Jesus, upon the fall of Satan, Adam and Eve, and one-third of the host of heaven. This is the original sin (Genesis 3:1; Ezek. 28, 31; Romans 5:12–21; Rev. 12:1-4; Deut. 32:7–8—v. 8, we are told in the Septuagint that the fallen angels become the nations of the world—"angels of God"—*ben el*—not "sons of Israel.").

God makes the earth formless and void, and re-makes the earth as a flesh age for the redemption and judgment of the fallen host. God is just, and will judge, but He also loves us, and wants to redeem/reconcile those who will love Him (Genesis 1:2, 3–2:3; Neh. 9:6; Isaiah 45:18; Matt. 18:14; Romans 5:10; Eph. 1).

God creates humans to replenish the earth. These are flesh beings, and may include the people of Nod (Gen. 1:28, 4:16).

God says the creation of heaven and earth and *all* the host of them are finished (Gen. 2:1). All is in reference to all things and all beings. Babies today are not new souls. All the beings of heaven and earth were finished by Day 6.

God removes Adam and Eve from Eden/Paradise, and banishes them to the re-created earth. Their spiritual, material, eternal body is replaced with a corrupt flesh body. They now must be born again, be redeemed/reconciled, in order to receive their eternal spirit back from God (Gen. 3:23-24; John 3:3-13; Heb. 2:17).

The offspring of the generations of Adam and Eve are flesh, and each is a body conceived by God to enable the fallen host an opportunity to be born again.

Each of us, the fallen children of God, in order to be redeemed must trust only in God/Jesus, God the Son. Thus, after being born physically, then, we must be born again with the eternal spirit of God. Unless we are born again (receive our eternal spirit—John 3:6—develop a relationship with God), our spirit stays with God, awaiting God's judgment at our death (Matt. 12:32). Each child must make a choice to trust Jesus, or not (Exod. 20:4; Job 38:4–7; Jer. 1:5; Hosea 1:10; Matt. 25:41; Luke 19:10; John 1:11–13, 3:5, 13, 17:5–6; Romans 3:25–26, 8:8–11, 16, 19-21, 29–30, 11:2; Gal. 4:6; Heb. 2:14–17; Rev. 12:1–4; 1 John 2:2, 4:10, 5:6–8).

Now that we understand the creation, the fall, and God's plan of predestination, the fallen host of heaven will now enter into this flesh age as babies, hopefully to be reconciled to God.

CHAPTER 11

GENERATIONS OF THIS AGE OF GRACE

Genesis 4:1—Eve is deceived (just as we are), and believes Satan is the Lord, and bears child number one:

"**A**dam and Eve" (man and woman), are ejected from Paradise, and are now deceived on the renewed earth also. This is the first use of the name Adam to refer to a specific individual.

In Revelation, many are deceived, as Satan arrives first on a white horse, *imitating* Christ (Rev. 6:1). In Genesis 3, Satan deceived many (see also Rev. 12:1–4).

Satan is continually *imitating* Christ (Isaiah 14:12; Eph. 6:11).

Eve's remark: "I've gotten a man from the Lord" is interpreted by some scholars as: "I've gotten a man, *even* the Lord." She thinks she bore the Messiah (as Mary bore Jesus—a unique creation by the Holy Spirit for the Spirit of God to dwell in). Some think she mistook Satan for God, as Satan is continually imitating God.

Genesis 4:2—Eve *continues* and bears child number two:

Twins? In the Hebrew, the word *again* can mean "continued," indicating twins. Many suggest that this was part of Satan's plan to destroy the plan of God to one day bring forth the Messiah, the Savior.

Genesis 4:2—Abel—-a keeper of sheep, and Cain—*server* of the ground:

In Hebrew, the word *tiller* is actually *server*. Cain does not serve the Lord. He serves worldly things, and the prince of this world, Satan.

Genesis 4:3–8— Cain and Abel reach maturity and give their offerings to God. Cain's is rejected; Cain kills Abel:

They both bring their offering at the same time. Are they both the same age? Are they twins?

Cain's offering is of his works and was not a blood offering, which God explicitly required as a covering for our sins. God caused a death to cover the sin of Adam and Eve with an animal skin (a blood sacrifice). Blood is God's command to cover our sins. Works by our hands are not acceptable. Adam and Eve used leaves to cover themselves (Gen. 3:7), but God requires a blood sacrifice from us, as flesh beings (Gen. 3:21).

Abel tended sheep—but why? They did not eat meat until the time of Noah (Gen. 9:3). Clothing could come from the plant harvest. Skins of animals are not necessary. Animals were necessary for the blood sacrifice. In Romans 5:13–14, we are told that all are condemned to death because of sin, even though those generations from Adam to Moses were not guilty of sin (the law having not been given yet). Therefore, the sin they are guilty of, is their sin in Eden. Abel, in Genesis 4:2, kept sheep for sacrifice to cover sin. So, obviously they were guilty of some sin in the past, because they were not guilty of sins listed in the law given to Moses (Romans 5:13–14, see *Original Sin* section).

Genesis 4:9–26 —Cain punished by God. Cain took a wife in land of Nod. Generations of Cain begin.

Cain's wife comes from *other people* created on Day 6? Most say she came from the family of Adam and Eve. Some Hebrew scholars say the people created on Day 6 are these people of Nod (see Genesis 1:26–27). It works either way.

Genesis 4:14: "*Everyone that findeth me.*" Some think that Cain was afraid of *other people* created on Day 6 (see Genesis 1:26–28), not his own family. Again, it works either way.

Hebrew scholars have suggested that these "*other people*" were not Adam and Eve.

Randall Isaac, executive director of the American Scientific Affiliation (with over 1,600 members), states that the human population began with around 10,000 humans—the DNA are clear on that. Science points to many people being part of the original human population, and the Bible can be read either way. Either there were just two people (Adam and Eve), or there may have been many people created on Day 6 of the creation, resulting in various species of humans, which have since interbred resulting in today's various races.

Genesis 5:1–6

Generation of Adam and Eve:

The word *book* (in Hebrew, *sefer*), means a *written* account. The Hebrew record, in written form, pre-dates Moses.

No mention of Cain here as a descendent of Adam. Note that the *seventh* generation in the line of Cain is Lamech, the murderer (Gen. 4:17–24). Today, we are actually in the *seventh* millennium of humans on earth according to many scholars, and this is the age of murder, with most violent deaths in America due to abortion. Many other lines are listed, but Cain is deliberately placed in a separate lineage (1 Chron. 1:1).

The *seventh* generation in the line of Seth is Enoch, and God "*took him.*" Meaning, he didn't die (Gen. 5:24), which suggests that perhaps during this *seventh* millennium, God will take those who trust in Him to heaven for eternity, as described in Revelation. The seventh day lists no night (Gen. 2:1–3).

"*In the day that God created man.*" This is a reference to Day 6 in *this* age (Gen. 1:26–28). Whereas, Adam and Eve were formed "*in the day the Lord God created the earth and heaven*"—Eden (Gen. 1:1, 2:4).

The old earth age (Eden), *became* formless and void—*tohu wabohu* (Gen. 1:2), as a result of the fall of man in Eden. The generations of man and woman are those born to Adam and Eve in this earth age in which we currently live.

In Genesis 5:1, "Adam" (man), is in reference to the father of all generations.

"*In the day they were created.*" These created on Day 6 were a new creation (flesh), created especially for this age of redemption—to bear children. Man was originally created, in Eden in a supernatural body. And now, for this age, there is the need for originally created (*bara*) *flesh* beings in order to replenish the world. These men and women either join together with Adam and Eve (as previously discussed in Genesis 1:26–31), or God establishes this original human flesh couple as "Adam and Eve," in order to bear children, and replenish the earth. Either way, humans "born of water" (born of a natural birth), must also be "born again" (John 3:5–7). Note that when we are "born again," we actually receive our spirit—verse 6. We become spirit, as well as flesh. We become a living "soul" (Gen. 2:7; John 3:6).

Genesis 5:1–2 is a repeat description of Genesis 1:26–27. This is the creation (of man and woman for this flesh age, made, in God's image, meaning using the *already existing* characteristics (image), of God.

Genesis 5:6–32—Generations of Adam—Seth to Noah:

Adam and Eve were transformed from the supernatural, and given mortal bodies of flesh.

Seth to Noah. Note that Seth was in the image of Adam and Eve. Whereas, Adam and Eve are in the image of God. Adam was called a "*son of God*" (Luke 3:38) and we are called "*sons of man.*" However, we can become sons of God again, by being "born again" (John 3:5–7).

Enoch did not die (Rev. 11:3–4).

Genesis 6:1–2; 4–6—Fallen angels who follow Satan and stay with Satan, deceive women on earth:

"*When men began to multiply on the face of the earth*" refers to how the population was exploding during these days of Noah, just before the flood. Just as today, where it took from the flood of Noah until AD 1865 to reach one billion people on the earth, the population is currently growing at the rate of 250,000 each day (Matt. 24:37).

God here describes Satan's effort to control this earth age for himself, and destroy God's plan of redemption/reconciliation for all the fallen souls who are predestined to be redeemed and reconciled. Satan's plan is to destroy the bloodlines, or generations of humans. Births from these unions are the source of "giants" and demons, which are different from the evil heavenly host (see Gen. 7:21, re: demons). The host in *heaven* do not marry, it does not say they can't unite with women on earth (Matt. 22:30; Mark 12:25; Luke 20:35).

Genesis 6:3—120 years will be for humans:

We are flesh, *not* as the "*sons of God*" (*bene ha-Elohim*), in verses 2 and 4. We are born into this flesh world, and take on flesh bodies.

Some scholars interpret this 120 years as God using Noah to spread the truth of God for a period of 120 years before the flood (1 Peter 2:5, 3:18–20), while others suggest that from this point, God will only give man 120 years to surrender to Him.

Genesis 6:4–6—Giants, Sons of God, mighty men, men of renown. Evil continually.

God's Word tells us that many people have encountered angels and didn't even know it (Hebrews 13:2). They appear as human as you or I. Perhaps this has happened to you or someone you know. Jesus appeared to people *after* His death and resurrection in His resurrected body (John 20:19). He was even able to materialize through walls—all supernatural—yet, He appeared human (John 20:24–29). We are told that we will be like the angels and Jesus, in the resurrection to come (1 Cor. 15:49; 1 John 3:2).

So, on the one hand we welcome the prospect of becoming like the angels. On the other hand, in Eph. 6:10–13, Paul tells us to be prepared to battle this world's darkness—the spiritual forces of evil from heavenly places. Here, we learn that some angelic forces are out to destroy our relationship with God.

The Bible reveals some pretty strange events in Genesis, and warns us that strange events will occur again in the end times.[66] In Matthew 13:52, Jesus tells us that the true student of the Bible understands and values both what is *old* (Gen. 6:1–4), and what is *new* (2 Thess. 2:3–10). Jesus also warns us of what is future (Matt. 24:37–39). God tells us in Genesis 3:15, that the seed (generations/DNA) of the woman would bring forth the Savior, Jesus, to eliminate Satan and sin. The sacrifice of Jesus was predestined before the foundation of the world (Rev. 13:8). We also read in Genesis 3:15, that the seed (generations/DNA), of the serpent (Satan) would try and ruin the plan of God. The battle continues (1 Tim. 4:1–10).

Satan's initial plan was to destroy the seed (generations/DNA) of the human race so that Jesus could not be born. To do this, some of Satan's angels came to earth (Jude 6–7), to begin populating the earth with giants/hybrids (Gen. 6:1–4—*Nephilim/giants, gibbor*). These hybrid giants' DNA would corrupt the DNA genome of future generations of humans. God's Word tells us the angels in *heaven* do not marry, but God's Word also tells us that angels did come to women here on *earth* (Genesis 6:1–4; Matt. 22:29–30).

The flood of Noah was necessary because the corruption had spread to everyone except Noah, who was perfect (spotless) in his *generations* (DNA— Gen. 6:9).

Notice that after the flood, this same problem was taking hold in the Promised Land (Gen. 15:18–21), and God instructed Israel to destroy all of them (Deut. 20:17–18). Satan was destroying the human population, and therefore, God commanded Israel to destroy the hybrids (giant) nations.

There are three Hebrew words to identify giants—*nephal, rapha*, and *gibbor*. The Bible gives numerous references to the generations of these various giants, beginning with the grandson of Noah—Nimrod (Gen. 10:8—*"mighty one"—gibbor/*giant). Nimrod led eventually to Amraphel and the Rephaites (Gen. 14:1–5—*rapha/*giants) at the time of Abram. Other great families were the Amakin, descendants of Amak (Num. 13:21–33—*Nephilim/*giants), the Ammorites, also known as the Zamzummins (Deut. 2:19–21, 3:11—*Rephaim/* giants), even up to Goliath and the Philistines (1 Sam. 17:51—*"champion"*— *gibbor/*giant).

God warned Israel not to mingle or intermarry with these nations, and instead, to destroy them, as these nations were the source of the Nephilim/giants (Lev. 20:2–5).

Jesus warned us that as in the days of Noah, the corruption of human flesh will occur in the last days. Note that since the time of Jesus, that evil has been restrained (2 Thess. 2:3–10).

All ancient cultures from all over the world have stories concerning the zodiac, dragons (dinosaurs), spirit beings or angels coming to earth, giants, and a great flood. The common source of all these stories would be Noah, whose generations spread to all parts of the world—including Noah's grandson, Nimrod, a giant who started a pagan religion in the land of Babylon (Genesis 10:8–10; Rev. 17:5).

Giants (*gigantis, gigas*, or *genenes*) in the Septuagint, means "earth-born" (part celestial, part terrestrial in origin), "under," "beneath," "inferior," "fall short," or "lacking." In other translations, the Hebrew word (*nefeel*, or *nephel*), is used, which means "fallen ones," or something fallen (an untimely birth, miscarriage, abortion, bully, tyrant, cast down, cast out, or a fallen giant). In Num. 13:28–33, and Deut. 3:11, they are described as being large (giants). These are the children of the fallen angels.

These fallen angels were of superior knowledge and power. Humans were warned not to begin to worship them. They came directly to this age without being birthed into the earth

In the original Hebrew text, references to these "sons of God" is *not* to humans, but to angelic beings (Job 1:6, 2:1, 38:7; Luke 20:35–36). Jewish historian Josephus wrote in *Antiquities* 1.3.1, concerning this passage that. "Angels accompanied with women and begat sons." This was also the view of both the Hebrew, and the *early* Christians, until the fourth century (when it was determined that this understanding seemed too much like the Egyptian and Greek myths of supernatural beings). Of course, those myths were a result of perverting the true salvation message (*originally* given in the zodiac by God, and passed down to Noah's children)—just as modern teachers are making excuses for *this* story of Satan's evil plan given in the Bible.

Normal usage of the term *sons of God* is to the host of heaven, and even the earliest Greek translation of the Hebrew, the Septuagint, translates *bene ha-Elohim* as referring to angels, the host of heaven. There are some who hold to the theory that *sons of God* here in Genesis) refers to the common title given to kings, or others, of great stature. It is true that this term is commonly applied to an *individual* in leadership, as an honorary title. Jesus was called "The Son of God."

E. Kantzsch, in "Gesenius '*Hebrew Grammar*', states *ben* (*of beni ha-elohim*) properly means "beings of the class, or tribe, of *Elohim*," not "sons of God," because "sons" actually refers to "adherents." Whereas, *ben* denotes membership. The Jewish priests were totally opposed to pagan polytheistic stories about gods, and yet, they translated the Hebrew sons of God as angels in the Septuagint. These angels are now chained (2 Peter 2:4; Jude 6).

The children born to these unions of angels and women, were called the Nephilim, or giants. These became the sources of demons. Biblically, this could be the reason that God saw total depravity in mankind—due to sex with foreign beings resulting in an infected and corrupted DNA.

The word for *men* in verse four, "*men of renown*" is the Hebrew word *enowsh*, which is not the normal Hebrew word used for men in these passages. *Enowsh* means mortal, weak, wicked, and blood thirsty.

The Hebrew book of Enoch records that the original blood drinkers were the Nephilim. Vampire stories are traced to the Nephilim. Satan makes the sacred blood sacrifice a mockery by using these vampire stories as a mock "imitation" of the sacrifice of Jesus.

Secular science is reporting studies in 2012 and 2013, which show possible interbreeding between "modern" humans and the Neanderthals, and Denisovians (other possible related species).[65, 73] This supports the biblical understanding of one pair of humans at the beginning producing several human species as the generations passed, and these various species have all eventually interbred producing todays makeup of various races.

Jesus tells us that the end times will be "*as in the days of Noah*" (Luke 17:26–30). Daniel 2:40–43 also hints at some similar event when *they* shall mingle with the seed of men in the end times. Will there be another attempt to destroy the bloodline/genome of humans in the end times "*as in the days of Noah*?

Note that Paul, in 1 Corinthians 11:10, states that women must cover their heads with *authority* because of the *angels*. Wearing a veil, and covering her head, expresses her authority over any fallen angel, as she is putting her trust in God's order and ways, and not submitting to any angel (Gal. 1:8–9).

Genesis 6:6–7—In Hebrew, *repented*, or *sorry*, actually means that God took a deep breath (sigh)—it *grieved* (pained) Him. God was not sorry; He was grieved.

Genesis 6:7–13—God will destroy life on earth—not Noah—Noah is *perfect*. In verse 8, Noah found grace in the eyes of the Lord. Grace is *unmerited* favor. Noah is faithful, but *not* perfect in his righteousness.

Noah *is* perfect in generations, in *bloodline* from Adam. In verse 9, *blameless*, or *perfect* is "without blemish," and, *in his generations*, or *in his time* is *in his descent*, or *family history*. The Hebrew word for *perfect* is *taman*, which means "without blemish"—a reference to *physical* purity.

It is not mentioned that Noah's family was perfect—just Noah.

There were eight in the ark. If one of the seven had been corrupted, even in previous generations by the "*sons of God*," (the fallen angels), then Satan's corruption continues into the world, even after the flood (Gen. 6:4; Num. 13:28–33; Deut. 3:11; Acts 17:26).

God pronounced an end to all flesh life, not the spirit, or breath of life (Gen. 6:12-13). It was the flesh bloodline of humanity which Satan had destroyed—except for Noah.

Genesis 6:14–22—Ark made—two of every kind—fowl, cattle, creeping thing

Two of those from the original creation of Genesis 1:1, which were *re*-made during the 7-day creation.

CHAPTER 12

THE FLOOD AND DEMONS

Genesis 7:3—Seven of every kind of clean beast and fowls of the air

Seven of those from the seven-day creation, which are newly (originally) created for this age (such as the winged fowl of Gen. 1:21).

These newly created animals, new and "clean," will be unblemished, and therefore, worthy of sacrifice to God by Noah, and he will need seven of these.

Genesis 7:15—Breath of Life

This is *not* the same breath of life given to Adam and Eve. This is the Hebrew word for normal breathing, a different Hebrew word than that used in Genesis 2:7 for the spirit of eternal life. However, the Hebrew word used in Genesis 7:22 *is* the spiritual, eternal breath of life. These fallen host who were corrupting the earth are now bound (2 Peter 2:4), and while their offspring's bodies were destroyed in the flood, the spirits that possessed these offspring were rejected by God (Jude 9). Today, these are the demon spirits which need a body to possess. They are being restrained until the end times (Zech. 5:5–11; 2 Thess. 2:3–10).

Genesis 7:17—Flood

The word *flood* in Hebrew here, is *mabbul,* a unique word meaning "cataclysm." There are eight other Hebrew words to describe floods which are local (rivers, or streams, lakes). Josephus, places the date of the flood at 2,262 years after the beginning of Adam on the earth. [39] Seventy percent of Earth today is covered with water. If the land were flat, there is enough water to cover the entire planet to a depth of 7,500 feet—about a mile and a half. [65]

Note that many historians believe that the Hebrew account of creation, and the flood of Noah to come later, are taken from other cultures, such as the Babylonian myths. However, just the opposite is true. The oral stories (possibly written), which Noah passed down, were actually the foundation for the Babylonian myths, as well as many others, and these oral/written stories were eventually written down in the Hebrew we have today, recording the words that God gave to Moses. Just because the *existing* Hebrew writings (parchment) do not date as early as the Babylonian tablets (clay), this does not mean that the Hebrew account was taken from the Babylonians—Just the opposite. The Babylonians, as well as many others, took the accounts of the creation, and of Noah, and made a story to fit their mythical gods. They perverted God's story.

In fact, John D. Morris, PhD, has reported on an earlier Babylonian tablet from the city of Nippus (Nippur), which dates to 2200 BC, soon after the flood and centuries before the famous *Gilgamesh* tablets, which date to 700 BC. This earlier tablet also records the flood story, and it agrees with the biblical account.

Demons—Evil Spirits
Genesis 7:21–24

Angels are often confused with demons. Many people equate the two, meaning that many people believe that demons are fallen angels. And, because of this confusion, many believe that because demons are spirits with no bodies, that angels are also spirits with no bodies.

Demons are spirits (spirit only). The word *demon* actually means "evil spirit," and demons need a body to possess (Mark 5:1–20). Angels have a supernatural body. Paul tells us in 1 Corinthians 15:40–44, that there are earthly bodies and heavenly bodies. Humans, when resurrected, will be given a supernatural body like the angels. Supernatural bodies have properties that allow them to go through walls and doors (just as Jesus showed). Therefore, the supernatural body has transparent qualities when needed.

So, if demons, which are evil spirits, are not fallen angels (which have bodies), then, where did these evil spirits come from? God's Word tells us in Genesis 6 that when angels came to Earth and took human women, the resulting children were called *Nephilim* (be sure and read the discussion in Genesis 6 about this, because up until the fourth century, this was the understanding of both the Hebrew and *early* Christians, and is still the basic understanding of the Hebrew). These Nephilim children (according to Scripture in Gen. 6, Num. 13:28–33, and Deut. 3:11), possessed great powers, and were called giants—referring to both their stature and their abilities. God's created beings, the host of heaven, sons of God, angels, humans, and stars, which possess both a spirit (the breath, or wind of life—that quality of eternal life), and a body—either earthly (flesh), or heavenly (supernatural). Angels have a spirit and a supernatural body. Humans have a spirit and a flesh body.

The Nephilim, however, are not clearly defined in God's Word. It would seem they are flesh bodies, born to human women, but possess *no* spirit, because the only beings created by God with an eternal spirit are the host of heaven. These Nephilim are born *after* the beings of creation were finished (Gen. 2:1); therefore, the understanding by many is that some fallen angels, rather than be punished by God (Jude 6—they did not follow God's plan of reconciliation), chose instead to abandon their supernatural bodies, and abandon heaven, for the bodies of these Nephilim (flesh) beings, and exist amongst the humans. Because of this corruption, God sent the flood, and killed all the children and babies in order to eliminate this corruption. All flesh was destroyed in this flood. This means that these eternal spirits (evil spirits—demons), now are in need of a body to possess (Mark 5:1–20). The demons are those spirits of the fallen angels who gave up their supernatural body, and since the flood, are now disembodied (in need of a body). Demons, therefore, are the *spirits* of the fallen angels who defied God's plan of reconciliation (birth to a flesh body).

Even at the time of Jesus, these evil spirits were common. But, since Jesus' time these demons have been "restrained" (2 Thess. 2:6–10), until the end times. There is a reference to the Nephilim, even after the flood, and it is theorized that either one, or more of Noah's son's wives, were corrupted, or possibly that other fallen angels must have tried again to corrupt the earth, after the flood. These Nephilim were destroyed by Israel as they entered the Promised Land, as they were commanded by God to kill all, even the babies, in order to destroy these giants. The last giant was killed by David (Goliath).

CHAPTER 13

AFTER THE FLOOD OF NOAH

GENESIS 8: 1–22

The Ark Journey

Genesis 8:1—*remembered*—God acted on the basis of a promise.

Genesis 8:3—The water receded for 150 days. The ark rested (a new beginning) on the same day of the same month, on which Christ rose from death, which is the Feast of First Fruits today.[66]

Genesis 8:4—The seventh month became the first month (Exod. 12), upon deliverance of Israel from bondage (the first Feast—Lev. 23), and the seventeenth day becomes the day of first fruits at the time of Christ.[66]

Genesis 8:7–12—Noah sent out a raven, and then a dove, and then another dove, until the dove found land.

Genesis 9:1—Replenish the Earth:

Replenish, refill the earth. The same Hebrew word as was used in the 7-day creation of Genesis 1:28. Again, babies are to be born, in order that they may hopefully be "born again" (John 3:1-7), and return to Paradise (Eden). The path back to Paradise is through being born flesh (to die), and being "born again."

Genesis 9:3–4

Eating of meat acceptable . . . not the blood:

God now allows humans to eat meat, but not to consume the blood—the life (Lev. 17:11). Why this change? In the world before the flood, mankind was involved in what Paul describes will also happen in the end times. Those who wish to keep humans away from worshiping the Creator provide humankind with alternatives (other ways), and these alternatives involve commitment to certain pagan actions. In 1 Timothy 4:1–3, Paul describes the "doctrine of demons," which will prevail during the end times. These include the forbidding to marry, and the requirement not to eat meat, and these practices can also be traced to the very beginnings after the flood (perhaps even before the flood—Gen. 6).

Concerning marriage, Nimrod is credited with forming celibate orders of priests which the Babylonians later also adopted. God's plan was to see people marry each other and raise children to worship Him—flesh (mortal) humans who would receive the truth of God, and receive their spirit (John 3:6), and who would die (Gen. 2:17). Satan's purpose was to destroy God's plan (destroy human flesh), and marriage was therefore promoted as something to do with your spiritual god (the angels—Gen. 6). In the pagan belief, a person who marries another human being does not elevate themselves. In order to elevate oneself and enter a higher plain, a person needs to marry a higher being . . . an angel, or god. Biblical marriage of one man to one woman is seen in pagan circles as idolatry, placing of the flesh above the spirit. This pagan ideal still exists in our own culture today.

In the end times, just as Jesus tells us that evil will rise again (Matt. 24:37–39), Paul is also telling us that there will be those who hold to marring only the higher order of spirit beings, and to deny marriage to another human—a return to the "days of Noah." Satan wants to have it both ways concerning marriage . . . either by denying marriage to another human through pagan practices, or by perverting God's plan for marriage with same sex unions, or polygamy.[67] Satan's purpose is to destroy the means of saving the host of heaven who fell, who need to be born flesh (mortal), hear the truth of God (Romans 10:13–17), and then be "born again" (John 3:1–7). Without God's plan of marriage, the plan of salvation is corrupted (Gen. 6).[67]

Concerning the eating of meat, we can look to the ancient teachings of the Hindu and Buddhist faiths, which require a person not to eat flesh. This is due to the pagan belief in reincarnation, and the belief that you might be eating a person re-entering life in the form of another animal, or insect. Another pagan belief is that when one dies they become part of all of nature (live on in oneness with nature--pantheism). When God allows humans to consume meat, it is a way of doing away with Satan's pagan teaching of reincarnation, as mankind enjoys these foods and ignores the pagan ways.

The Hebrew book of Enoch records that the original blood drinkers were the Nephilim. Vampire stories are traced to the Nephilim. Satan makes the sacred blood sacrifice a mockery by using the vampire image as a mock imitation of sacrificing one life to save another. God forbids consumption of blood because life itself (being sacred), is represented in the blood (Lev. 17:11). Blood (life) is the sacrifice of Jesus to cover our sins.

Genesis 9:13–16
A Bow in the Clouds:
God uses a rainbow to remind us of His covenant with us.

Some scientists theorize that it didn't rain on the planet before the flood of Noah and the convulsions of the Earth's surface associated with the flood (see Gen. 2:5–6). The Earth, prior to the flood of Noah, was more uniform. It didn't have the great mountain ranges we see today. It was continually covered with a thick mist, which kept the earth moist, and kept harmful ultraviolet rays out. In fact, science has determined that all the great mountain ranges we have today, actually were created by some cataclysmic event. They were all created at the same time. And, further, that the Earth was all covered by a worldwide flood, up to 800 feet higher than today's sea levels.

This was reported in several places, including a special edition of *Scientific American* in 2005. Of course, scientists quoted in this article speculate that this worldwide flood occurred millions of years ago; whereas, the Bible tells us this occurred during man's time. Additionally, scientists in *Acts & Facts*, February 2011, state that erosion rates far outpace the conventional scientific view of millions of years of plate tectonics and mountain formation. The mountains we see should have eroded away, millions of years ago, if conventional science theories are maintained.

When we study the scientific evidence, and the biblical record, the only real difference between them is *time—age*.[65]

Genesis 9:18–27
Canaan Cursed:
A child of Satan's seed? Only Noah was perfect. Ham's line was cursed by grandfather Noah (1 Chron. 2:55; Matt. 13:38–39, Matt. 23:31–33; John 8:44; 1 John 3:10, 12). Both Canaan, and Nimrod (Babylon) are in Ham's line.

Note that Canaan (Ham), is singled out in verse 18, and this is where the Nephilim were eventually found at the time of the Exodus (Num. 13:28–33—see Gen. 6 section).

The ancients in positions of authority (like Noah) had a robe that indicated his position of authority. Ham reported that his father was naked. Evidently,

Ham desired his father's authority, and took his robe to embarrass him, and elevate himself. Ham reported to his brothers that their father was, in effect, not worthy of his status. Satan, also, wants to take God's authority, and deceives many to follow him, rather than God (Rev. 12:1–4).

CHAPTER 14

NIMROD AND THE QUEEN OF HEAVEN
GENESIS 10–11

Genesis 10:8–10
Nimrod of Babylon: Noah's Grandson

False religions and idol worship are traced to Nimrod, and continued to the Phoenicians with Baal, and the Samaritans with Ishtar, and Egypt with Isis, and Rome with Venus, and many others (Rev. 17:1–7). Nimrod was referred to as a "giant" ("mighty"/*gibbor*/giant—see *Gen. 6* section).

The earliest known stone monument site is a massive structure showing a focus on religion and the afterlife. The location is very close to where Noah would have landed . . . in Turkey. Called Gobekli Tepe, this site is featured in an article titled "In the Beginning," in *Biblical Archeological Review*, January 2013. This site pre-dates all other sites in the world, including the Great Pyramids in Egypt. Because this ancient site is in Turkey, and because animals carved into the stone are not native to the area, it lends evidence that man's earliest structures and civilizations originated at the very place where the Bible tells us man first established his presence after the flood of Noah, and the animals being released.

The Great Pyramids of Egypt were actually built *before* any other pyramids.[65] Note that even though the Great Pyramids existed when the events of both the Old and the New Testament, took place in Egypt, the Bible makes *no* reference to these great wonders of the world. These structures are viewed by many as a product of Satan, the giants, and the Nephilim in an attempt to imitate God's new heaven and earth, and therefore God never gives them recognition in His Word, even though Egypt is central to the biblical accounts in both the Old and New Testaments.[66, 67]

Future generations, as well as Nimrod, are influenced by the Queen of Heaven - The Moon Goddess

Revelation 17:5 refers to all false teachings when it refers to "The Great Harlot," the false religion, or worldly type of church.

What is the Mystery? Why Babylon? Who is the Woman?

The cultic worship of mother, child, and fertility goes back to the earliest writings. From the very beginning, even in Genesis 10:8–10, one finds reference to the beginnings of this false worship, with the reference to Nimrod, who with Semiramis and her son, Tammuz, have fostered many forms of cultic worship through the centuries, all based upon God's story in the Zodiac These include Anu and Ishtar birthing Tammuz at the time of Israel (Jer. 7:18, 44:17–19, 25), and they lead eventually to Egypt with Osiris, and Isis birthing Horus, the Egyptian copy of Tammuz.

These mythical deities were all based on rites of fertility. Even today, many celebrate Easter as a season of fertile springtime. In ancient Samaria, this spring celebration involved the exchanging of Ishtar (Easter) eggs. Further, the son of this goddess (Tammuz), was supposedly resurrected to life in these mythical legends. As one looks through history, one finds numerous imitations of God's plan, which put either some person (such as Nimrod—a giant), or Satan, or this world, at the center of attention, instead of God.

Whether one is a Protestant, Catholic, or any faith, God tells us the only path to God's kingdom is by trusting in Jesus. Jesus claimed He, alone, is the way (John 14:6). Jesus gave us eyewitness evidence of His power over death (1 Cor. 15:1–8, Acts 1:1–8). Jesus welcomes all who will trust in Him. Many have put their trust in Jesus and will be welcomed into the kingdom of heaven. There are also many who call themselves Christians who are not truly born again (John 3:3–7). Even though they think of themselves as pretty good people, and go to church, their priority in this life is not Jesus. Jesus Himself said that they will not be welcome in God's kingdom (Mat. 7:21–23, Matt. 25:1–13). The key to the kingdom of God is trusting in Jesus.

In the ancient world, the mythical deities were first defined by the Sumerians (Babylon—people of the East). The Sumerians, the first literate civilization, worshiped the moon goddess, which was called by many names, including Nanna, and Suen. This was the dominant goddess of the Fertile Crescent. Later on, the Akkadians (Semite peoples), took the name Suen, and transliterated it to Sin. Thus, Sin became the favorite name for the moon goddess throughout the ancient Fertile Crescent. From the very beginning, the crescent moon was the symbol of the moon goddess (female). Sin is also viewed as a male god in other areas, and at different periods of time, as will be explained in the following pages.

Later still, the Egyptians would become the defining force, followed by Greece (with its capital at Babylon), and then Rome at the time of Christ. All these empires had their mythology rooted in these Babylonian (Eastern) deities, and the moon goddess Sin. In the city of Ur (Abraham's home), ancient tablets list the primary deities as An (the male god), and Inanna, or Nammu (the Queen of Heaven). The Stella of Ur-Nammu (the female goddess—Queen of Heaven), has the crescent moon placed at the very top of the register of gods, because the moon goddess was the highest of gods—*not* the male, as would be the case in Egypt and Rome, centuries later.[41]

In Sumerian mythology, the origin of the whole universe was due to Nammu, the water goddess. From her waters was birthed all we see, including all the male gods.[46] This is an imitation of God's creation, where the waters were divided. One of these births was to the moon goddess Sin. In Mesopotamia, the female goddess was dominant, until animal husbandry and domestication later became established, and only then, did the male god figure begin to dominate in some cultures. But, in Mesopotamia, where Abraham came from, the pagan male gods were still a servant to the Mother Goddess of all creation. The Mother Goddess was considered unmarried, and in some locations, a virgin. It was the re-productive power of the earth which was associated with the Mother Goddess (Mother Earth), and which was of paramount importance in agricultural life in the ancient world.[46]

As agriculture became controllable, the male dominance of heavenly deities took hold. Sin came to be seen as a male moon god, which became later known as Al-ilah (the highest of gods), in the Arab world, hundreds of years after Christ. Even so, Sin still retained a female form (Al-lat—the female moon goddess). In the Sumerian explanation of gods, a god could also be a goddess. This has confused scholars for centuries. But, the origin of this male/female change can be cleared up by studying Greek (Western) myth. The Greek Empire, which came much later, established its capital at Babylon, and adopted many of the pagan practices of Babylon. Greece has given us better records of these mythical deities' origins, and how this moon god (male), could be also known as a moon goddess (Queen of Heaven).[41, 46]

All this mythology is a product of perverting God's Word from the very beginning. God, in Genesis 2:21–24, tells us how God first created man (Adam). Then, "out of man," God made woman (Eve—the bearer of life). In the Greek myth, Zeus (equivalent of Adam), produces Hera, the female goddess. Hera is not born to Zeus, but she comes "out of him" (just as Eve comes out of Adam). Therefore, in the ancient Babylonian myths, a god could become a goddess. In the Greek myth, Hera became known as Athena after a great flood. Athena, the mother goddess, is usually pictured with the serpent. The serpent is central to mythology in *all ancient cultures all over the world*, due to the fact that, as in the Babylonian and Greek understanding, it was the serpent who gave man knowledge, which was previously restricted to only God (Gen. 3:1–5). The Sumerians at Babylon began a false worship, where the serpent became the source of knowledge, and worship was given to the serpent, and to the moon goddess, the bearer of life.

All of this Greek myth is actually rooted in Babylon, the capital of the Greek Empire at the time of Alexander the Great.

In the Greek (Western) understanding, the moon god Sin, became a female goddess and became the highest of gods. This was brought about in mythology as the result of the earth goddess, Inanna, becoming the Queen of Heaven (as well as the Queen of Earth), due to her marrying many other gods, including Anu, the primary male god. She became the moon goddess with resurrection power, thus, replacing the male moon god Sin. Later still, the moon goddess was once again viewed as a male (Al-ilah—the highest of gods), at the time of Mohammad, 650 years after Christ.[46]

As the Sumerian origins gave way to the Semitic culture, these deities' male names became (depending upon the area of the world you lived in), Nimrod, Marduk, Assur, and Ba'al. The female names became Semiramis, Inanna, Ishtar, Astarte, and Ba'al-Ti. Many of them had a child called Tammuz. Tammuz, son of Inanna (Semiramis, Ishtar, Astarte, et cetera), was considered a god. He was supposedly resurrected in these myths, after his death, but he was always the earthly servant of the Mother Goddess of the universe. The Assyrian counterpart of Inanna was Ishtar, the Queen of Heaven and Earth. The Queen of Heaven, and the Mother of Earth was the dominant deity, due to her acts of renewal and regeneration.

The kings of Mesopotamia were often regarded as subservient to the goddess, because (unlike Egypt, with its predictable cycle of flooding for agriculture, which the pharaohs could predict), the river waters in Mesopotamia were unpredictable—indicating the kings had no power. Thus, all worship was directed to the Queen of Heaven, who was also the Mother of Earth—not the male kings, or their male deities.

The Old Testament rebuked the worship of the moon god (Deut. 4:19, 17:3).

Over time (as men gained control over agriculture and animal husbandry), the sky god (the sun), was seen as the greater, more powerful of gods—controlling seasons, and weather, and war. However, the Mother Goddess, being associated with the moon, as well as the earth, was still venerated as a source of life and rebirth.

As time progressed, the moon goddess, combined with Isis (from Egypt), and became known as Namaia. Eventually, male dominance caused a return to the worship of the moon as a male god (Sin), once again. In time, Sin became Al-ilah (a title meaning highest deity). Montgomery Watt, in the *Journal of Semitic Studies* (Vol. 16: "Belief in a High God in Pre-Islamic Mecca"), states that this moon god/goddess, was the primary god of Ur. This is where Abraham lived (around 2000 BC). Nabonidus (555–539 BC—over a thousand years before Muhammad), the last king of Babylon, built Tayma, Arabia, as a center of moon god worship. The Arab tribes always remained steadfast in worship of the moon god, Al-ilah. In fact, Mecca was built as a shrine for the moon god.[46]

At the time of Muhammad (around AD 650), this moon god Sin, was seen as married to the sun goddess. Three stars of heaven were his daughters: Al-Lat, Al-Uzza, and Monat—all considered high gods. The moon god was *named* Sin, and his *title* was Al-ilah (the highest god), which became Allah. Muhammad declared that Allah was not only the greatest god, but the only god. This was due to a vision Muhammad received, that the main god of his city (Al-ilah—the moon god), was the one, true God, symbolized by the crescent moon today, for Islam, as well as the Wicca, and Mother Earth faiths.[33]

To this day, the Muslim faithful fast during the ninth month on the Islamic calendar, which begins and ends with the appearance of the crescent moon in the sky.

Centuries later, in Egypt, the ancient Tammuz myth becomes the story of Osiris, Isis, and their son Horus. Many ancient myths (including the Tammuz myth), seem to parallel the story of Christ's virgin birth, resurrection etc. These myths were elevated to historical status in the late 1800s and the early 1900s. Recent scholarship has, however, shown that each of these myths fall far short of being historic parallels. Author Lee Strobel has provided evidence showing these myths have been either later embellished to relate to Christ, or were actually created after the time of Christ.[59] Historically, these myths in no way even closely relate to the life of Christ. We must remember that the original story of the virgin, and the resurrection, were given in the zodiac, by God, which has been perverted into these other myths.[66, 67]

After the time of Christ, all the variations of the Mother Goddess—the Queen of Heaven (whether called Ishtar in Mesopotamia, or Asherah, Anat, or Astarte in Syria, or Isis—which means "She of many names," in Egypt), all of these had formed into the universal female goddess, a beautiful virgin, generally known as the "Queen of Heaven."

Today, supernatural apparitions of a glowing woman (a bright light), are occurring at increasing intervals, all over the world. The last fifty years has seen an explosion in these appearances. The apparition claims to be Mary, Mother of God. She speaks through people; sometimes through several people at the same time. These apparitions have been documented, and in some cases, recorded on film. Millions of people worldwide now claim to have witnessed an apparition. These signs, wonders, and miracles, are causing mass conversions, and life-changing experiences.

Jesus performed signs and wonders, such as changing water to wine (John 2:1–11), walking on water (Matt. 14:22–33), eyewitness evidence of which is given in the Bible. Jesus also fulfilled over 300 prophecies, written hundreds of years before His birth, as recorded in the Old and New Testaments by actual eyewitnesses.

The Mary apparition claims signs and wonders, such as changing silver to gold. In fact, many such instances have been testified to, and recorded.

Jesus healed many, and raised people from the dead, and eyewitness testimony is given of these miracles in the Bible.

The Mary apparition claims to heal people. In fact, many healings have been documented and recognized by various churches, including the Roman Catholic Church.

In John 14:6, Jesus said that He was the way, the truth, and the life, and that no one would enter the kingdom of heaven, but by Him.

The Mary apparition asks people to read their Bible, pray every day, trust in Jesus. She says she has been appointed by the Father, and her Son, to save all nations, bring unity of the faiths, and global peace.

Peace—Love—Unity. Sounds great, but is it?

In 2004, the last two popes, as well as many other Roman Catholic leaders, in light of these great signs, wonders, and miracles, formally dedicated the entire world to Mary. They are trusting in her to bring unity between all faiths, as well as global peace. This is because Jesus is too controversial and divisive (Jesus is a judge, and will divide and separate—Luke 12:49–53), and He did *not* come to bring peace.

God tells us to test all things—1 Thess. 5:21.

The apparition of Mary says she is the mediator *and* intercessor, between God and us. The Roman Catholic Church has proclaimed Mary as "intercessor." In 1854, she was declared "Mary the conqueror of death and evil."

Hebrews 7:25 declares that Jesus is our Mediator/Intercessor.

First Timothy 2:5 states that there is one God, and one mediator—Jesus.

The apparition of Mary says she is our *advocate*, sent by the Father and Son.

1 John 2:1says Jesus is our Advocate.

Luke 1:47–48: Mary called Jesus *her* God and Savior.

The apparition of Mary says she has been sent to save the world. She says she, alone, is able to redeem us, and the world. She describes herself as the "ark of *salvation.*" The Roman Catholic Church declared Mary as the "Ark in Heaven" in 1950.

First Peter 1:18–19: Jesus is our Redeemer.

John 14:6: Jesus is the only way to salvation.

Luke 1:38: Mary says she is the Lord's servant.

Acts 4:11–12: Jesus is the only way to salvation.

Hosea 13:4: God only—no human.

The apparition of Mary says she is ever-present to receive our prayers, and intercede for us. She is omnipresent. She is a co-redemptorist, able to redeem us apart from Jesus. The Roman Catholic Church is very close to proclaiming her the co-redemptorist. On August 16, 2007, the Pope said: "Mary's glorification in her virginal body is the confirmation of her total solidarity with the Son, both in the conflict, and in victory…she is from all eternity…one and the same decree of predestination . . . the noble associate of the divine Redeemer . . . as Queen, she sits in splendor at the right hand of her Son."

John 14:6: No one but Jesus.

Isaiah 47:4: The Lord is our Redeemer.

Isaiah 45:21–22: One God—no other (Isa. 45:5–6, 44:6–8; 1 Cor. 8:4).

Acts 4:11—12: Jesus is the only Redeemer.

Luke 11:27–28: Jesus said that others are as blessed as Mary.

The apparition of Mary says she atones for our sins, and suffers for us (as her heart and Christ's heart are one—and they suffer together for the world's sins). In 1950, the Roman Catholic Church proclaimed that Mary had gone to heaven as Jesus had—the "Assumption of Mary."

John 19:30: Jesus said, "It is finished."

First Peter 3:18: Christ suffered once for all.

Hebrews 10:12–14, 18: One sacrifice—no longer any suffering.

The apparition of Mary claims to be sinless—an immaculate conception. She claims also to have ascended bodily into heaven, and is seen now as the "Bright and Morning Star." She will crush the serpent. The Roman Catholic Church proclaimed Mary as a "perpetual virgin" in AD 553, and proclaimed Mary an "Immaculate Conception," and "sinless," in 1854.

2 Corinthians 11:14–15: Satan is an angel of light.

Romans 3:23: All are sinners (Mary also).

Acts 1: Jesus ascended, bodily, into heaven.

Genesis 3:15: Jesus will crush the serpent.

Revelation 22:16: Jesus is called the Bright and Morning Star.

Isaiah 42:8: God will give His glory to no one.

Isaiah 44:6: God is the first and the last, beside God there is no other.

The apparition of Mary says statues and shrines are to be erected to her, and to be honored and venerated, as a reminder of her presence. A statue is under construction now, which will be twice as tall as the Statue of Liberty. In 431 AD, Mary was proclaimed "Mother of God." In 1854, Mary was named the "Queen and Gate to Heaven," by the Roman Catholic Church.

Deuteronomy 4:14–19: No idols, no statues, no heavenly wonders are to be worshiped.

Isaiah 42:8—God will give His glory to no one.

The apparition of Mary often appears with a baby.

First Peter 3:21–22: Jesus was bodily resurrected as a man—not as a baby. He is now alive as the God-Man.

The apparition of Mary says she is to be called the Queen of Heaven, Mother of God, Queen of the Ages, the Lady of all Nations. She says that when she is declared by the church to be co-redemptorist, that she will bring unity under one holy church and peace to the world. The Roman Catholic Church has declared her the "Lady of All Nations," in 2005, in addition to all the other names, and the church is expected to proclaim her co-redemptorist in the near future.

First Thessalonians 5:2–3: Peace, then sudden destruction.

Daniel 8:25: Peace, then destruction.

Daniel 9:27: A peace covenant, then destruction.

Revelation 6:1–4: A white horse (peace), then a red horse (war).

Daniel 7:23: Unity of the nations, but devoured.

Revelation 13:7–8: Unity, to be followed by death.

Revelation 17:18: Unity, under a false religion.

Revelation 18:3: Unity, under a false religion which is doomed.

Second Timothy 3:13: Imposters will deceive.

Second Thessalonians 2:9–10: The lawless one, with counterfeit signs and wonders, will deceive those who refuse the truth.

Matthew 24:24: False prophets with great signs and wonders, (such as to deceive the very elect), will arise.

Galatians 1:8–9: Reject even an angel who does not agree with God's Word.

2 Corinthians 11:14–15: Satan is an angel of light.

First Timothy 4:1: In the end times, some will follow deceitful spirits.

How is it possible for Mary, the Queen of Heaven, to be the Lady of Nations—to bring global peace, and bring unity to all faiths in the world, (including Islam, and Buddhism, and Hinduism, etc.)?

It turns out that, just as it is described in God's Word (Jer. 7:18, 44:17–25; Ezek. 8:14) concerning the Queen of Heaven, (who was worshiped, going back as far as 4,000 years ago, in Mesopotamia), this same "Mother of All Nations" has been venerated by many nations for all these years, (with the exception of those who follow the Bible). Of course, today, even many of those who call themselves Christian, have begun to accept the Queen of Heaven as the way to unity and global peace, including the largest Christian organization in the world—the Roman Catholic Church.

What about Islam? Chapter 19 of the Qur'an is actually named after Mary. Islamic tradition is that Jesus is to have said that Allah has exhorted Him (Jesus), to honor His mother, who purged Him of vanity and wickedness. In chapter 21, of the Qur'an, Allah says he breathed into Mary his spirit, to make her a sign to all mankind. Islam venerates Mary as a pure and holy saint, even above Muhammad. The Qur'an says Muhammad must ask for forgiveness for his sins.

Apparitions of Mary have, in fact, appeared to millions of Muslims, and they have experienced healings, and they are in ever-increasing numbers making pilgrimages to Mary shrines in Iraq, Syria, Egypt, Turkey, and others. In chapter 66, of the Qur'an, Allah said he gives Mary as the faithful example for all the world's believers to follow.

It is the hope of the pope, as well as many others, that Islam will join Catholics in unity, under the veneration of Mary. To this end, the Roman Catholic Church has declared that the god of Islam, is the *same God* recognized by the Roman Catholic Church, according to the Second Vatican Council, Lumen Gentium 16, November 21, 1964, and restated by Pope Benedict's address in Cameroon in March of 2009.

How about Hindus, Buddhists, Taoists, and others, including faiths of the New Age, and even Wicca? The primary deities of all these world religions has always included veneration of a female goddess (commonly called the Queen of Heaven, or Mother of Earth). This goddess is loved, because she is a goddess of life and birth, and she transcends nations and prejudices. She is welcomed by all nations, because her message is global peace, unity, and tolerance.

One of the most unexpected developments since the birth of Christ 2,000 years ago is the re-birth today of the religion of the Queen of Heaven—the Mother Goddess. Buddhists revere, and adore a female figure, which dates back to early times in India.

The Hindu faith has always revered the female goddess. The Chinese goddess is known as Kwan-yin (the Goddess of Mercy), who brings the faithful to heaven. In Japan, she is known as the goddess, Kwan-on, the Mother of Mercy. In Japan, even converted Christians accept that their Kwan-on, is in fact, the foreshadowing of the goddess Mary.

So, it turns out that peoples of all nations are being won over to the peace, love, and unity promised by the Queen of Heaven. Al, but one. Notice, that one nation in all the world has, and does, treat the Queen of Heaven as evil wickedness (especially since in their history, they, too, once worshiped her, they suffered for that worship). Now it becomes clear why Jerusalem and all of Israel, is a trouble to all the world. Furthermore, any nation which supports Israel will be in direct opposition to the apparition, and to her followers, the nations of the world who desire peace and unity.

The history of the Queen of Heaven has common threads for all nations, from the beginning of recorded history, going all the way back to Jericho, the oldest of cities.

Babylon had a Mother Goddess cult. A primary god, Anu (a male), was god over the entire universe. But, he shared power with the Mother Goddess, Nammu. She was credited with actually creating the universe for him to govern. Eventually, Nimrod (Gen. 10:8–9) established himself as a god on Earth. After his death, he was called Ba'al (the sun god). Nimrod's wife Semiramis, became the moon god with rebirth powers (seen as moon cycles). Certain religious practices, which began in Babylon, spread to all nations, and are with us, even today, in the Christian church. The Greek myths derive from these Babylonian roots (Babylon was the capital of the Greek Empire at the time of Alexander the Great), and they have preserved a record for us of how these mother-child cults relate to God's creation, the fall, and the serpent. Man embraced the serpent as the provider of knowledge. Ancient Mesopotamian clay tablets tell us their creator-god was depicted as a serpent (the god of knowledge).

Jericho had a goddess cult, a Mother Goddess deity. Archeologists have uncovered much evidence of this in the form of statues and figurines they place at 7000 BC. Nineveh also had a female deity figure venerating maternity, a Mother Goddess.

Iraq, where Abraham came from, had a temple dedicated there to the Mother Goddess, Inanna-Ishtar, and her son, Dumazi-Tammuz, as far back as 3800 BC. Iran and Elam also had a female goddess statue on the Acropolis, dating to 3000 BC

Jericho, around 3000 BC, was venerating skulls, and had linked the Mother Goddess to the land of the dead and Mother Earth. Egypt, around 2000 BC, worshiped Seth, as the son of the earth god and the sky goddess. Egypt worshiped the sun god as the sustainer of life, but also worshiped the sky goddess as the producer of life, and also of reproduction.

Mesopotamia saw many transitions in their gods, until their primary gods of worship finally consolidated and became Sin (the moon god or goddess—usually female, but sometimes male, depending on the local culture); Shamash (the sun god—male), and, Adad (the storm god—male). The most important of these was the moon goddess—the crescent moon.

Greece, as early as 1000 BC, worshiped the Queen of Heaven (Athena), who was given authority by the serpent. Athena was worshiped as mother of all. Greek myth states Kronos (Chronos, or time), and Rhea (earth), united to form the first man Zeus (similar to Adam's creation by God). In the Greek myth, Hera comes out of Zeus (similar to Eve coming out of Adam). This is an imitation of the Genesis creation, except that the Greeks worship the serpent, who gave man knowledge to become gods themselves. Later, the goddess Hera, reappears after a great flood, as Athena, and she receives power from the serpent. Athena and the serpent are worshiped by the Greek Empire as the mother goddess. This Athena (goddess of the serpent), is given authority over the Sphinx, a winged lion with the head of *a woman*. The wings represent power over the heavens, the lion represents power over the earth, and the woman represents power over life.

Many cultures in ancient history had stories they passed down through the centuries concerning the woman of heaven (a virgin), as well as her child (and his death and resurrection), and the judgment, and salvation of humankind. This image of the virgin and child has been with mankind ever since the creation when God created the stars and named them (Job 38:32).

In the oldest book of the Bible (Job—2150 BC), considered by many to be the oldest book in human history, verse 38:32 refers to the *Mazzaroth* (Hebrew for constellations of the Zodiac), as well as several individual constellations. *Zodiac* means "The way," or "The path," in both Hebrew and Sanskrit. In other words, a picture of the way of salvation.

In all the ancient nations, the *same* 12 constellations, in the same order, with the same images (pictures), are referenced as far back in antiquity as we can go. There must be a common source.

It has been pointed out by scholars (including the historian Josephus), that the original source for the zodiac is God's gospel. It was given to Adam and Eve, and passed down thru the generations of Noah, to the seventy nations. In the Arabic tradition, these signs in the heavens are said to have come from Seth and Enoch. Genesis 1:14 states that God gave us the stars for signs: 12 constellations, 12 tribes, 12 apostles (see also Rev. 12:1). God named the stars (Psalm 147:4; Isaiah 40:26). But, it is also noted that God's gospel story in the heavens has been perverted, just as the Bible today is being perverted by many. The term *seventh heaven* (used by Islam and many others), refers to the five planets, the sun, and the moon, each forming a crystal sphere, with the Earth at the center (second century, Ptolemy). This is false. The Bible refers to a third heaven (2 Cor. 12:2), which agrees with our scientific understanding of the air, the stars, and the unknown beyond the expanse of the universe.

When one looks at the zodiac, one may question where to start, in this story in the heavens, because all the constellations are in a circle. By going to the oldest zodiacs, one of which is found in the Egyptian Temple of Esneh (4,000 or more years old), the Sphinx pictured there points out where to start. The Sphinx head (a woman's head, is toward Virgo the virgin, and the tail, toward Leo the lion. Modern astrology has perverted the zodiac, and the pagan story now begins with Aries the lamb.

Throughout the history of these ancient cultures, there is a common reverence of a life-producing Mother Goddess. She was the dominant figure in the ancient Near-Eastern religions. All of these cultures share a common source for worshiping her—namely, the zodiac. However, if one actually studies the ancient names given to the individual stars and constellations by God (Psalm 147:4, Isaiah 40:26), it becomes clear that the original story in the stars actually agrees with the message in the Bible; not with the various other stories told by other ancient cultures.

Israel was forbidden by God to worship the stars and the Queen of Heaven. However, King Ahab became a worshipper because of his wife Jezebel, and her priests of Baal. Archeological evidence shows that soon after Solomon's time, the Astarte sanctuary (the center of the goddess cult), stood next to the temple of the God of Israel (Jer. 7:18, 44:17–25; Ezek. 8:14).

In Revelation 12, John gives us a picture of a woman (symbolic of the betrothed to God—the bride—all the host of heaven—some of which became Israel), bringing forth a Savior (Jesus). The woman is standing on the moon (the moon under her feet), meaning that sin is conquered.

God's Word warns us about the Queen of Heaven (a different woman):

Isaiah 47:1–7: A virgin Queen of Nations—daughter of Babylon.

Revelation 18:3–7: A queen of all the nations—wicked.

Isaiah 47:9–11: The queen will meet her end. Note that the false prophet will be eliminated by the beast in the very end. The beast will exalt himself (Dan. 11:4–5, Revelation 17:16).

Zechariah 5:5–11: A wicked woman in Babylon.

Revelation 18:2–3: Wicked Babylon, a woman.

Revelation 2:20: The harlot, Jezebel, is tolerated, which is a sin to God.

First Kings 16:31–33: Jezebel worships the Queen of Heaven, called Asherah.

Daniel 11:36–37: Desire to worship the Queen of Heaven. The desire of people for the woman-queen.

First Thessalonians 2:3–12: Before the day of the Lord's return, apostasy comes. First the mystery of lawlessness, which is already working in the world with signs, wonders, and deceptions, for those who do not love the truth.

Isaiah 47: The wicked woman hides (verse 10). A mystery. Judged in the end times.

Zechariah 5:6–11: The wicked woman is hidden—hidden until the end times.

Revelation 17: The wicked woman is the mystery of Babylon—a great harlot—false religion.

Matthew 13:33: Evil is hidden by the woman. The whole world is corrupted (leavened). Three measures (or pecks), equals one ephah, which is supposed to be the offering to God, but it is leavened, puffed up, not pure, defiled).

Zechariah 5:6–7: One ephah holds evil..

First Thessalonians 5:21: Test all things.

In the ancient world, at the same time this false religion is spreading across the globe, over a period of 1,800 years (according to Scripture), the earth itself continues to break apart.

Genesis 10:25
Earth divided in days of Peleg:
This is possible Earth-crust displacement, where the single land mass (which science calls Pangaea), splits.[65]

The Hebrew form of the word *palag* refers to an *ongoing* event of division, not a one-time event. Scripture indicates that Peleg's parents gave him a name to reflect the ongoing division of the lands—something happening during "his days."

Sea levels rose 4,000 to 5,000 years ago and buried large areas of land mass all around the world. Many catastrophic events occurred as the Earth surface changed. Since this period 4,000 years ago, there have been several mini ice ages, and subsequent warming periods. The Bible tells us the earth broke up dramatically over an 1,800-year period.[65]

Genesis 10:32
Nations divided:
Families and tribes spread out into the whole earth as the Earth continues to break apart.[65]

Genesis 11:1–9
One Language Confounded:
God divided them because of pride, wanting to be like God themselves, so as to preserve at least one group for true worship.

Note that in verse 1, the word *speech* in Hebrew means "creed," or "confession." In verse 2, the word *journeyed* in Hebrew means "pulled out," or "abandon."

The King James says, "from the east." The "east" is associated in Scripture, with rebellion against God. They were either coming from a point of view of evil (east) to build a tower, or they were heading toward evil (east)—and thus, away from God (Gen. 3:23–24, 4:13–16).

Note that the trees (beings), and man, were placed in the "*east*" part of Eden. God foreknew of their rebellion (Gen. 2:9).

Scientific studies reported in 2006 concerning mDNA (mitochondrial DNA), which scientists estimate to have a specific mutation rate, demonstrate how humans migrated across the globe. These studies (reported in *Science*, in *Newsweek*, Feb. 6, 2006, as well as numerous other places), provide evidence that man (Eve), originated in the East-African/West-Arabian area, and from there spread to the *east* (including Australia), and then west to Africa, north to Europe, and eventually, the Americas. Except for the time periods speculated by scientists, these findings agree exactly with the biblical accounts of how people would have spread from the landing of Noah, throughout the world, first moving east.

So, this is Puzzle Piece # 1: Are the creation accounts of both Genesis 1, and Genesis 2 and 3, two accounts of the same creation event? Or, two accounts of two different creation events? And, if these are two separate creation events (the Hebrew position), then, which came first? Have past generations of scholars forced this piece into a wrong place, where it only seems to fit?

Having determined that these two accounts are indeed separate, and since science has forced us to take a closer look at our paradigm, of these creation events of God, it now seems correct to understand that the Eden account is the account of original creation, and the fall of the host. Furthermore, this Eden account actually precedes the seven-day account, (this age we now live in), which is the period of reconciliation back to God for those who will trust in Christ—or a death sentence to hell for those who deny Christ.

Puzzle Piece # 2: Predestination is now understandable, because we can understand how God's sovereignty, as well as our freewill, and personal responsibility, have all been preserved. We used our free will in Eden, and God in His sovereignty is willing to sacrifice to save us.

Puzzle Piece # 3: Original Sin is now understandable, because it is clear from this understanding of these two creation events—that we sinned in the original creation—Eden. That is why we are sinners at conception, even in the womb, because we are personally responsible for our own sin. Now we are born of water (flesh), and, hopefully, all will be "born again"—John 3:5–7. God did not have to do this, but this is how much God loves us—John 3:16, 17.

Puzzle Piece # 4: The Millennium. There are many views of the millennium. There are many ways scholars are trying to fit this puzzle piece of God's Word into the picture.

Where does it really fit? Ironically, this millennium period is also related to this understanding that there were two creation events—that we sinned in Eden, and are now born into this period of reconciliation. The millennium will be a time of gleaning to gather those who have never been called by Jesus to salvation. This is not a second chance. God is just, and He will make sure everyone has an opportunity to hear the gospel message (Romans 10:13–17).[66, 68]

PREDESTINATION SCRIPTURE LIST

Are we *Totally depraved*, or, are we basically good, and just need to fix up some areas in our life to be saved? Are we able to choose God?

Psalm 14:1–3: God looked, and no one does good, not one, none seek, or understand God.
Matthew 19:17: Only one who is good—God.

Mark 10:18: Only one who is good—God. Luke 18:19: Only one who is good—God.

Romans 3:10–18: None good, no one understands, none seek God, not one.

Romans 3:23: All have sinned.

Romans 11:32: All are bound over to disobedience, so God might offer mercy to all (but without God's leading, we do not seek God).

1 Corinthians 2:14: Those not born again consider God's truth to be foolishness.

Philippians 2:21: We seek our self, not Christ.

Did God provide **U**nconditional election, or, is there a *reason why God chooses some, and rejects others?*

Genesis 3:8: Some fallen were ashamed and hid. These are cursed, but elect.
Genesis 3:14: Some are hostile to God, not ashamed, and these are cursed, and damned to hell.

Joshua 24:15: Choose for yourself whom you will serve. We are commanded to choose, even though it is God who gives us the faith needed to choose Him. We confirm our disobedience, or our love.

Psalm 135:6: God is sovereign over all actions of men.

Proverb 21:1: God directs the ways of the heart of man.

Isaiah 46:9–10: The end is declared (predestined) from the beginning, *from former things long past.*

Ezekiel 18:23: God takes no pleasure in the death of the wicked.

Rather, God is pleased when they turn from their ways, and live. We are all sinners, and some are saved because they love God, because He gives them faith. Others continue to deny God.

Matthew 15:13: God the Father chooses.

John 1:12–13: God gives us the right to be His. This is *not* of man's will.

John 3:16: God loves the whole world. God loves us all. However, many do not love God. These will be divorced (see Study on **Marriage and Divorce**—[67]).

John 6:29: God provides us with belief/faith.

John 6:37–44: The Father gives some to be saved. Those given by the Father will be raised up to salvation. No one comes to Jesus, unless the Father draws them. Some say these verses are in the context of only the Jewish leadership. However, verses 24 and 40 both place the context to everyone.

John 6:64–65: God the Father chooses.

John 15:16: God chooses us; we do not choose Him.

John 17:6–9: God gave some to Jesus—Jesus does not pray for others.

Acts 13:48: God appoints (ordains) who is to be saved.

Romans 8:14: God leads the chosen to salvation.

Romans 8:28: God calls some to fulfill His purpose. Paul uses the past tense for called, justified, and glorified. Paul is speaking of those in histories past, who are now glorified, those who led to Jesus fulfilling God's purpose (verse 28).

Romans 8:29: God foreknew some (foreloved some, *not* foresaw), and predestined some, so that the Savior would fulfill His destiny.

Romans 8:30: And, these elect God called, justified, and glorified (past tense).

Romans 9:11:12: Salvation is God's choice and purpose.

These weren't yet born. They hadn't done good or bad in this world, yet one is loved, and the other is hated (Mal. 1:1–5). Some say the context of Chapters 9–11 is to Israel, and not to individual people, and this is to tell us that salvation is not a birthright of Abraham, nor a reward for keeping the law. However, anyone can be grafted into the tree of salvation who has faith, Jew or Gentile. Predestination is God's choice before our birth, and God provides the faith, which is needed, to those to be saved. God extends mercy to both, Jew and Gentile equally (Romans 11:32).

Romans 9:14–18: Salvation does not depend upon man's will, but upon God (verse 16). But, God is just, God is not arbitrary (verse 14).

1 Corinthians 2:14: Those not born again, consider God's truth to be foolishness.

Ephesians 1:4: The elect are chosen and predestined, before the foundation of the world.

Ephesians 1:11: The elect are predestined to receive their inheritance.

Ephesians 2:1–9: We are dead in a relationship with God, but God reaches out to some. God has made the *provision* of salvation available freely to all (grace). But, many resist God, and persist in sin (Acts 7:51). Salvation is the free gift available to all, by the grace of God. However, God has predestined only certain ones to be given faith, which is required, in order to love God, and actually partake of His salvation (71) (see *Salvation "SAP"* Study at Target Truth Ministries.com).

1 Timothy 2:3–6: God "will have" (desires) all to be saved, even though He knows many do not love Him.

1 Timothy 4:10: Jesus is the Savior of all, especially believers, meaning that He *makes provision* for all, but only believers who actually love God, will actually receive salvation (those who receive faith, the elect).

Titus 2:11: The grace of God brings salvation to all, meaning that God *makes provision* for salvation for all, but only will give faith to some—the elect.

Titus 3:5–6: We are saved by God. We do not save ourselves.

James 2:26: We are *dead* in a relationship with God (without our spirit from God).

2 Peter 3:9: God does not wish for anyone to perish, but for all to come to Him (context is God's patience, *not* that everyone, even the unbelievers, will be saved).

1 John 2:2: God loves the whole world (meaning Jew and Gentile, equally). Propitiation means His sacrifice is *sufficient* to satisfy the wrath of God against the whole world, *if* the whole world would love God.

1 John 4:10: We did not love God. He loved us.

1 John 4:19: We do not love God 1. God 1 loved us.

Is *the atonement of Jesus Limited*? Or, did Jesus pay the debt for all people's sins, thus, making everyone whole? Or, did Jesus make provision (sufficient enough) for the salvation of all?

Isaiah 53:11–12: *Many* will be justified (not all), and He will bear the iniquities of the *many*. He bore the sin of *many*.

Ezekiel 45:18–20: There will be blood sacrifices in the millennium, for the unintended sins of the non–elect (meaning that Jesus paid the price for all of the sins of the elect—those predestined by God to salvation in this age of reconciliation).

Matthew 20:28: Jesus is the ransom for *many*. Many will be saved.

Sin is not *eliminated* by Jesus' death. The sins are

covered, forgiven.

Matthew 22:11–14: The sins of some people are not covered. This is because they do not have faith.

Matthew 26:28: Jesus' blood is shed for *many*. Not all will be saved.

Sin is not eliminated by Jesus' death. The sins are covered—forgiven.

Mark 14:24: Jesus' blood is shed for *many*. Not all will be saved. Sin is not eliminated by Jesus' death. The sins are covered—forgiven.

John 10:11: Jesus died for the sheep (not the goats).

John 10:26: Some people *are not* His sheep (the goats).

John 17:6–9: God gives *some* to Jesus. Jesus does *not* pray for others.

Acts 13:48: God appoints (ordains) who is to be saved.

Romans 5:18: "all" men. Verse 19 states "many." Justification is made available only to those who have faith.

Romans 6:10: Jesus died *once* for all (all time). This is not a reference to people, but to His relationship with this age and His death, dying *once* for all time (see Hebrews 10:12).

2 Corinthians 5:14–15: Christ died for all (context is Christ's love controlling *all* the saved, *not* the unsaved "controls *us,*" "compels *us,*" the elect).

2 Corinthians 5:19: "world" (making "reconciliation" available), but only those who have faith obtain salvation. "committed to *us*" (elect).

1 Timothy 2:3–6: God *desires* all to be saved, even though He knows many do not love Him.

1 Timothy 4:10: Jesus is the Savior of all, especially believers (in particular, believers—"we" labor, "we" trust). This is a contextual reference to the elect, *not* to the non–elect. The term "Savior" implies *"preserver," "maintainer,"* as well as *"deliverer".* The non–elect need maintaining, until the judgment.

Titus 2:11: The *grace* of God brings salvation to all, meaning that God *makes provision* for salvation for all, by offering *grace* to all, but only will give faith to *some,* the elect (Eph. 2:8—salvation is the *gift* of God).

Hebrews 2:9: "everyone"—verse 10 states "many." "Tasting death" for everyone does not indicate salvation for everyone—only that salvation has been made available for those who will have faith.

Hebrews 7:27: We need forgiveness *daily.* Jesus died once for all (all *time*—see Heb. 10:12).

Hebrews 9:28: Christ offered Himself once to bear the sins of *many.*

Hebrews 10:12: Christ offered Himself once, for all *time.*

1 John 2:2: Jesus paid for the sins of the whole world (This is in the context of the world's *elect*). Romans 3:25–26 tells us that only those who have *faith* will be justified, not the whole world. The propitiation is made "available." However, only those who have faith obtain salvation. His sacrifice is *sufficient* for the whole world, but He died only for the *many* who will trust and love Him.

Is grace *Irresistible*? Or, does a person have free will to deny God, even if that person is chosen by God for salvation?

Matthew 5:45: God sends rain on the good and the bad.

Matthew 16:17: God reveals to us who Christ is.

Matthew 16:24: People must deny self, and follow God.

John 4:19: God 1 loved us, we did not 1 love God.

John 6:44–45: No one comes to Jesus, unless the Father draws them.

Some say that this is addressed to the Jewish leaders only, and not to all people. But, both verses 24 and 40, place the context to everyone.

John 10:26–30: The Father gives the sheep to be saved, and God's sheep will *never* be lost.

John 15:16: We do not choose God. God chooses us.

Acts 13:48: God appoints (ordains) who is to be saved.

2 Corinthians 13:4: God chooses who is to be saved.

Ephesians 1:13–14: The saved are sealed. Inheritance is guaranteed.

Ephesians 2:1–9: We are dead in our relationship with God, but God reaches out to some. God has made the provision of salvation available to all freely (grace), but many resist God and persist in sin (Acts 7:51). Salvation is the free gift, available to all, by the grace of God. However, God has predestined only certain ones to be given faith (which is required, in order to love God), and actually partake of His salvation (see *Salvation* Study at TargetTruthMinistries.com).[66]

Philippians 1:6: God, who began a good work in the saved, will complete the work.

Hebrews 12:2: God is the author and perfecter of faith.

James 2:26: We are dead in our relationship with God, without our spirit from God.

Perseverance of the saints? Or, can a person lose their salvation?[71] (see study on *Salvation* at Target Truth Ministries.com, where SAP—that sticky stuff—is the key to understanding).

Psalm 37:23–28: The Lord upholds the saved, will not forsake them, and will protect them forever.

Luke 12:42–48: If you return to the world's ways, you will be appointed with the unbelievers (one's faithfulness is the evidence of *truly* being saved. Those *not truly* saved will fall). The purpose of these warnings is to encourage even unbelievers to practice godly virtues.

John 5:24: No more condemnation for the saved, they have crossed from death to life.

John 6:37: All of these the Father gives to Jesus, Satan cannot take them out of His hand. Some say that this is addressed to the Jewish leaders only, and not to all people.

However, both verses 24 and 40 place the context to everyone.

John 10:26–30: God's sheep will not be lost.

Romans 6:23: The gift is eternal life in Christ.

Romans 8:1: There is no condemnation for those in Christ.

Romans 8:14: If led by the Spirit, you are a son of God.

Romans 8:39: Nothing can separate us. Paul says "I am convinced."

Romans 11:22: Must continue to struggle, or salvation will be taken away (those who are *not truly* saved—the unbelievers—will be cut off in the end). The purpose of these warnings is to encourage even unbelievers to practice godly virtues.

1 Corinthians 1:seven–9: God will keep the saved strong to the end—blameless.

1 Corinthians 3:10–15: The saved that are careless will suffer loss of reward in God's kingdom, but will remain saved—verse 15.

1 Corinthians 5: Cast out the immoral, do not associate with the immoral

(this refers to *so–called* saved people —verse 11. The *truly* saved will show shame, and be humble and submissive to God).

1 Corinthians 9:27: Paul cautioned about being cast away (*true* faith will be demonstrated in one's life. Even though we live in two natures, we will show shame in the flesh, and praise God for forgiveness. Those *not truly* faithful will be cast away).

1 Corinthians 10:12: Don't fall—be careful (the *truly* saved exist in two natures, but we are to endeavor to set an example of being Christ–like. Those *not truly* saved will fall). The purpose of these warnings is to encourage even unbelievers to practice godly virtues.

1 Corinthians 15:1–2: We must hold fast (the *truly* saved exist in two natures, but we are to endeavor to set an example of being Christ–like. Those *not truly* saved will fall). The purpose of these warnings is to encourage even unbelievers to practice godly virtues.

2 Corinthians 5:17: If in Christ, you are a new person.

Galatians 5:19–26: Those who practice these things cannot inherit the kingdom of God. The *truly* saved exist in two natures, and will show shame when in the flesh, in order to demonstrate evidence of being saved. Those *not truly* saved will fall. The purpose of these warnings is to encourage even unbelievers to practice godly virtues.

Ephesians 1:13–14: The saved are sealed—inheritance is guaranteed.

Ephesians 6:11–13: We need armor, or we could fail. The *truly* saved exist in two natures. We are to use the protection of the Holy Spirit in our lives. Those *not truly* saved will fall. The purpose of these warnings is to encourage even unbelievers to practice godly virtues.

Philippians 1:6: God, who began a good work in the saved, will complete the work.

Hebrews 6:4–8: If they "fall away," they cannot be renewed again ("fall away" is a term meaning "separate from," or "deny" Christ. Sinning is falling short, not denying God).

Hebrews 8:12: God will remember our sins no more.

Hebrews 10:38–39: Those who draw back into perdition are lost (they never were *truly* saved).

Hebrews 13:5–6: God says "Never will I leave you, never will I forsake you."

1 Timothy 4:1: Some depart from the faith (these never were *truly* saved—John 6:66—the disciples departed).
2 Timothy. 2:11–13: Must endure. If we deny, we lose eternal life (endurance is the evidence of our faith. Those who deny were *never truly* saved).

James 2:19: Satan walked with God. Satan believes in God, but will not *trust* in God (*true* faith is demonstrated by trusting in God. The unfaithful will be exposed).

1 Peter 5: Satan will devour, so be alert and resist (God does not tempt us, but we exist in two natures until we are resurrected to our new bodies. Resist Satan, and glorify God. Be an example to others).

2 Peter 1:10–11: God calls and chooses, but we still exist in the flesh, and will stumble, and are encouraged to yield to the Holy Spirit, so as to receive joy and peace of mind, abundantly.

2 Peter 2:20–21: If you escape the evil of the world, and then fall back, it is worse for you (there are degrees of rewards in God's kingdom).

2 Peter 3:17: Don't fall from steadfastness, beware of evil (the *truly* saved exist in two natures, and are encouraged to demonstrate the likeness of Christ).

1 John 2:18–19: Some are not "really" saved.

All Scripture to this point is part of appendix 1 predestined verses.

APPENDIX 2

CREATION COMPARISON CHART

MODERN CONVENTIONAL VIEW (GREEK – WESTERN) From the fourth century to today	HEBREW/EARLY CHRISTIAN VIEW (JEWISH – EASTERN) From the time of Jesus until the fourth century
God created the Heavens (plural) and the Earth (Gen. 1:1 – NAS, NIV).	God created the Heaven (single) and the Earth (Gen. 1:1 KJV).
God created the host (beings) of Heaven (*Job 38:1–18*; Psalm 33:6–9; Rev. 12:1–2; Eph. 1:4–5, 11)	God created the host (beings) of Heaven / Eden (Psalm 33:6–9; Rev. 12:1–2; Eph. 1:4–5, 11)
Earth *is* formless and void "*tohu wabohu*" (Gen. 1:2) (*But*, **Isa. 45:18** says earth was *not* created "*tohu wabohu*")	God gives the description of all the host (beings) of Heaven and Eden (Gen. 2–3; Job 33:4–6; Rev. 12:1–2)
The creation – a 7-day account (Genesis 1:3–2:3) (In this conventional view—Eden is part of day 6 of the 7–day creation account)	God gives the story of the fall of many beings. Sin enters Paradise (Eden) through Satan (Gen. 3; Ezek. 28:12–19, Ezek. 31; Isa. 14:12–19; Rev. 12:3–4).
Day 6—man and woman are created (Gen. 1:26–27) (*supposedly* Eden – *many conflicts* – Gen. 2:5–3:24)	Transition between creation accounts (Genesis 2:4) from Eden(paradise) to the 7-day account.

All creation, including the host (beings) of Heaven, and of earth, are finished (Gen. 2:1; Eph. 1:4–5, 11). (*Some believe babies born today are a new creation ?*)	The earth **becomes** formless and void "*tohu wabohu*"– (Gen.1:2; Isa. 45:12—earth re–made (*asah*) & mortal humans created (*bara*)—see also Isa. 45:18—earth **not** created "*tohu wabohu*"; also, Job 38:1–18 where host of heaven witness earth being *re–made*).
Transition between creation accounts (Gen. 2:4) from the 7-day to the Eden (Paradise) creation account (Gen. 2:5–3:24). Eden and the fall part of Day 6.	Adam and Eve, and 1/3 of the host, are all banished to the cursed earth (Gen. 3; Rev. 12:3–4).
Adam and Eve and others are banished to the cursed earth due to the fall (Gen. 3; Rev. 12:3–4). **The age of Grace begins.**	All creation, including the host (beings) of Heaven, and of earth, are finished (Gen. 2:1).Babies are *not* a new creation (Eph. 1:4–5, 11; Rom. 8:28–30).From the fallen host, Adam and Eve are selected to begin The Age of Grace.
Sin enters *this world* through Adam (Rom. 5:12)	Sin enters *this world* through Adam (Rom. 5:12).
God will establish the nations of the world according to the number of the fallen angels of God cast out to earth (Deut. 32:7–8 – *Septuagint*; Rev. 12:1–4)	God will establish the nations of the world according to the number of the fallen angels of God cast out to earth (Deut. 32:7–8 – *Septuagint*; Rev. 12:1–4)
This world is Satan's domain (Job 1:7; Matt. 4:8–10; Luke 22:31–32; John 12:31; Rom.8:20–22; 2 Cor. 4:4; Eph. 2:2; 1 John 4:4).	This world is Satan's domain (Job 1:7; Matt. 4:8–10; Luke 22:31–32; John 12:31; Rom. 8:20–22; 2 Cor. 4:4; Eph. 2:2; 1 John 4:4).
It is thought that children now born flesh receive the sin of Adam (Bible reference?). *How?Why?*	Children now born flesh are responsible for their own sin, due to their following Satan in Eden (Gen. 3; Rev.12:3–4; John 3:1–7).

Children are seen as innocent until some "age of accountability" (Rom. 7:9?). *Nevertheless,* death reigns (Rom. 5:14, 6:23).	Children are condemned at conception because of sin in Eden (Jn. 3:18; Rom. 1:21–32, 6:23; Psalm 51:5, Psalm 58:3; Rev. 12:3–4).
When we knew God, we denied God (Rom. 1:20–21).No one seeks God (Rom. 3:10–12). We are all dead in our relationship with God in this age (Eph. 2:1–5).	When we knew God, we denied God (Rom. 1:20–21). No one seeks God (Rom. 3:10–12). We are all dead in our relationship with God in this age (Eph. 2:1–5).
God leads some to salvation. Those not led, remain condemned (Psalm 14:1–3; Jn. 6:44–45,15:16—God chooses, not us). *What is the reason some are chosen to be saved?*	God leads some to salvation. Those not led remain condemned (Psalm 14:1–3; Jn. 6:44–45, 15:16).Some in Eden showed shame (Gen. 3:7–8), others contempt (Satan).
The elect cannot deny God . . . Jesus will not lose any (Jn. 6:39).	The elect cannot deny God...Jesus will not lose any (Jn. 6:39).
If "born again," we can be *reconciled back* into a relationship with God (Jn. 3:1–7; Rom. 5:10–11). *When did we have a previous relationship with God, which allows us to be reconciled back?* (Ezek. 31; Rom. 1:20–21; Eph. 1:4–5, 11; Rev. 12:1–4).	If "born again," we can be *reconciled back* into a relationship with God, based upon to our previous relationship with God in Eden (Jn. 3:1–7; Rom. 1:20–21, 5:10–12; Eph. 1:4–5, 11; Gen. 2–3; Ezek. 31; Rev. 12:1–4).
Summary – I am declared a sinner at conception, and must be "born again."Adam is responsible. *God is seen as arbitrary – the sequence confusing.* **Scriptural conflicts exist.**	**Summary** – I was created, and once was with God, but have fallen, and must be "born again" – I am responsible. *God is loving, forgiving, and merciful.* **Scripture agrees with Scripture.**

REFERENCES

1. Rendsburg, Gary A., PhD., Rutgers University, Jewish Studies Dept., History Dept., *The Book of Genesis*, The Teaching Company, 2006, Part 1, pg. 93-96,100, Part 2, pg. 114-115.
2. Rohl, David M., *Pharaohs and Kings*, 1996.
3. Edersheim, Alfred, *Sketches of Jewish Social Life*, Eerdmans, 1990.
4. Fitzroy, *Ancient Commentaries—Genesis*, Dearborn Pub. Chicago and London, 2001.
5. Fitzroy, *Ancient Commentaries—Romans*, Dearborn Pub. Chicago and London, 2001.
6. Humphreys, Dr. D. Russell, *Starlight and Time*, Master Books, Green Forest, AZ, 1997.
7. Schroeder, Dr. Gerald, *The Science of God*, Free Press of Simon and Schuster, 1997.
8. Francisco, Clyde T., *Introducing the Old Testament*, Tennessee: Broadman Press, 1997.
9. Mathews, Kenneth A., *The New American Commentary—Genesis* 111:26,Broadman and Holman Pub., 1996.
10. Ryrie, Charles C., *Basic Theology*, Chicago: Moody Press, 1999.
11. Harrelson, Walter, *Interpreting the Old Testament*, Vanderbilt Univ., 1964.
12. Plaut, W.G., *The Torah*, Union of American Hebrew Congregations, N.Y., 1981.
13. Baker, *In the Image of God*, Moody Press, Chicago, Ill, 1991.
14. Willis, *The Teachings of the Church Fathers*, Ignatius Press, San Francisco, Calif., 2002.

15. Bercot, *Dictionary of Early Christian Beliefs*, Hendrickson Pub., Mass., 1998.

16. Rendsburg, Gary A., PhD., Rutgers University, Jewish Studies Dept., History Dept., *The Book of Genesis*, The Teaching Company, 2006.

17. Enns, Paul, *The Moody Handbook of Theology*, Moody Press, Chicago, Ill., 1989.

18. Rendsburg, Gary A., PhD., Rutgers University, Jewish Studies Dept., History Dept., *The Book of Genesis*, The Teaching Company, 2006, pgs. 11-12.

19. Grey, Gorman, *The Age of the Universe* .

20. Eckman, David, Professor of Hebrew, Western Seminary.

21. Thomas, W.H. Griffith, *Through the Pentateuch*, Eerdmans, 1973, pg. 31.

22. Watts, J, and Smith, Billy, Baptist Theological Seminary, Nashville, Tenn.

23. Jackson, Paul N., *Redemption—a Word Study*, Biblical Illustrator, Vol. 31 #4, Lifeway, Nashville Tenn., Summer, 2005.

24. Francisco, Clyde T., *Introducing the Old Testament*, Nashville Tennessee, Broadman Press, 1997.

25. Selph, Rovert, *The Doctrine of Election—Southern Baptists*, Sprinkle Pub., Harrisonburg Va., 1988.

26. Harl, Prof. Kennith W, *Origins of the Great Ancient Civilizations*, Tulane Univ, The Teaching Co.,2005, pg. 67.

27. Anderson, B.W., *Introduction; Mythopoetic and Theological Dimensions of Biblical Creation Faith*, Fortress, Philadelphia, 1984.

28. Wakeman, Mary, *God's Battle with the Monster: A Study in Biblical Imagery*, Leiden, E.J. Brill, 1973.

29. Plaut, W.G., *The Torah*, Union of American Hebrew Congregations, N.Y., 1981, pg. 24.

30. Kantzer, Kenneth & Gundry, Stanley, *Perspectives on Evangelical Theology*, Baker Books, Grand Rapids, Mich.

31. Huges, R.Kent, *Genesis*, Crossway Books, Wheaton Ill. 2004.

32. Morris, Henry, *The Genesis Record*, pg. 164-168.

33. Burney, Gerry, *The Paradigm Trilogy*, Xulon Press, 2003—**burneyfam. com.**

34. Guthrie, Shirley, *Christian Doctrine*, John Knox Press, Atlanta Georgia, 1968, pg. 215.

35. Morris, John, Institute for Creation Science.

36. *Scientifi c American*, Special Edition on Earth, Sept. 2005, pgs. 26-27.

37. Showers, Renald, *Angels*, Friends of Israel, New Jersey.
38. Troitski, V.S., Astrophysics and Space Science, 1987, 139.
39. Sutterfield, Barry, Norman, Trevor, *Atomic Constants, Light and Time*, Flanders, University of South Australia, 1987.
40. Fisher, Loren, *Genesis—A Royal Epic*, Professor of Hebrew and Ancient Semitic Languages, Claremont Theological Graduate University.
41. Albright, William, *From the Stone Age to Christianity*, Doubleday— Anchor Books, Garden City, New York, 1953.
42. Erickson, Millard J., *Introducing Christian Doctrine*, Baker Books, Grand Rapids Mi, 2000.
43. Cole, R. Alan, *Galatians*, Eerdmans Pub., Grand Rapids, Mich., 1989.
44. Capes, David B., Biblical Illustrator, *Adoption in the First Century*, Lifeway, Nashville, Tenn., Vol. 31 # 5, Fall 2005.
45. Dockery, David, *Ephesians : One Body in Christ*, Convention Press, Nashville, Tenn., 1997.
46. James, E.O., *The Ancient Gods*, Castle Books, Edison, N.J., 2004.
47. Tetlow, Jim, and Oakland, Roger, and Meyers, Brad, *Queen of All*, Eternal Publications, Fairport N.Y., 2006.
48. Hisslopt, Michael, *The Two Babylons*.
49. Missler, Chuck, *The Sword of Allah*, Koinonia House, 1994.
50. Morey, Dr. Robert, *Is Allah of the Quran the True Universal God?*, faithdefenders.com, Orange Calif.
51. Moshay, G.J.O., *Who is this Allah?*, Dorchester House, Buks, U.K., 1994.
52. Jeffey, Arthur, *Islam, Muhammad, and His Religion*, Liberal Arts Press, New York, 1958.
53. Guilaume, Alfred, *Islam*, Penguin, 1956.
54. VanEss, John, *Meet the Arab*, New York, 1943.
55. Hall, Kevin, *Eden*, Biblical Illustrator, Nashville Tenn., Winter 2007-2008.
56. Rowley, H. H., *Job*, New Century Bible Commentary, Grand Rapids, Mi., Eerdmans Pub. 1980, pg. 30.
57. Byrne, Brendan, *Sons of God*, The Anchor Bible Dictionary, Vol. 6, Doubleday, New York, 1992, pgs. 156-159.
58. FitPatrick, Mary Ph.D., Wellmuth, John Ph.D., *St. Thomas Aquinas on Spiritual Matters*, Marquette Univ. Press, Milwaukee, Wisc., 1949, pg. 15.
59. Strobel, Lee, *The Case for the Real Jesus*, Zondervan, Grand Rapids, Mich., 2007, pgs. 157-188.

60. Lockyer, Herbert, *All the Angels in the Bible*, Hendrickson Pub., Peabody, Mass., 1995, pg. 127.

61. MacGorman, *Layman's Bible Book Commentary*, Broadman Press, Nashville, Tenn., 1980

62. Larkin, Clarence, *Rightly Dividing the Word*.

63. Telushkin, Rabbi Joseph, *Jewish Literacy*, Harper Collins, N.Y., 1991.

64. Unger, *Biblical Demonology*, Weaton:Van Kampen Press, 1967 pg. 48.

65. Burney, Gerry, *Science, Origins, & Ancient Civilizations—Scientific Evidence Withheld from School Textbooks*, Xulon Press, 2014.

66. Burney, Gerry, *Revelation, Apostasy, End-Times, & "This Generation,"* Xulon Press, 2013.

67. Burney, Gerry, *God's Plan / Satan's Plan*, Xulon Press, 2013.

68. Burney, Gerry, *Book of Chronologies & Time Charts*, BurneyFam.com, 2013.

69. Waskow, Arthur, *Seasons of our Joy*, Beacon Press, Massachusetts, 1990.

70. Walvoord, John, & Zuck, Roy, *The Bible Knowledge Commentary*, Dallas Seminary Faculty, Victor Books, Wheaton Ill., 1983.

71. Kasemann, Ernst, *Commentary on Romans*, Eerdmans Pub., Mich., 1980.

72. Hendrickson, *Dictionary of Early Christian Beliefs*, Peabody Mass., 1999, pgs. 141-5, 271-4, 284-5.

73. Hoggard, Michel W., *Giants*, Prophetic Research Ministries, Festus, Mo., 2012.

74. Mortenson, Terry, & Thane, Ury, *Coming to Grips with Genesis*, Master Books, Green Forest, AR., 2008.

75. McGrath, Alister, The Christian Theology Reader, Blackwell, Oxford & Cambridge, 1993, pg. 357.

76. McGrath, Alister, The Christian Theology Reader, Blackwell, Oxford & Cambridge, 1993, pg. 216.

ABOUT THE AUTHOR

Gerry Burney graduated from San Francisco State University with a degree in Interdisciplinary Studies, and pursued graduate study at the University of California, Berkeley, and seminary study through the Southern Baptist Seminary, Nashville, Tennessee. He authored his first book on economics and poverty in 1985. Mr. Burney is a veteran of the US Air Force, and served in Vietnam. He retired from managing microwave communication technologies for over thirty years. He has pastored in several Baptist churches within the Mendo-Lake association of churches in California, and is currently the chaplain to the inmates for the Mendocino County Jail and Juvenile Hall. He has been a high school teacher, and teaches seminars on biblical studies (also available on YouTube). He also operates an outreach to prisons (TargetTruthMinistries.com), with weekly studies sent via US Mail at no cost to prisoners.

CPSIA information can be obtained
at www.ICGtesting.com
Printed in the USA
LVHW01s1022131117
556086LV00001B/76/P